Jesus, Family, & Coffee

Tiffany Strebeck

Copyright © 2018 Tiffany Strebeck

All rights reserved.

ISBN:1719236100
ISBN-13:9781719236102

DEDICATION

This book is dedicated to everyone who pushed me to publish this book.

CONTENTS

1	ARE YOU A DAHLIA, OR A SNAPDRAGON	1
2	COULD I LAY MY ISAAC DOWN?	Pg #3
3	THERE ARE NO ORPHANS OF GOD	Pg #5
4	'RISE UP': A CALL TO WOMEN WARRIORS	Pg #7
5	TAKE THESE HANDS	Pg #13
6	REMEMBER THE LILLIES	Pg #15
7	LET ME WALK WITH YOU JESUS	Pg #18
8	HE KNOWS ME	Pg #21
9	A WALK WORTH IMITATING	Pg #24
10	I KNOW WHO I AM	Pg #24
11	LET HELL'S GATES RATTLE	Pg #27
12	THE RAINBOW REMAINS	Pg #29
13	I'M NOT SATISFIED	Pg #32
14	LIFE AFTER THE COMMA	Pg #35
15	HIS TIMING BRINGS BEAUTY	Pg #37
16	I'M GOING FOR GOLD	Pg #41
17	I'M DESPERATE FOR YOU	Pg #44
18	I CAN'T COMPLAIN	Pg #47
19	MARY'S SACRIFICE: A CHRISTMAS DEVOTION	Pg #49

20	WHAT WOULD MY TREASURE CHEST HOLD	Pg #52
21	SPEAK LIFE TO YOUR DRY BONES	Pg #54
22	THE STEADY HAND OF GOD	Pg #56
23	KEEP SINGING	Pg #58
24	I WILL NOT BE MOVED	Pg #60
25	THE FORGOTTEN PART OF JOB'S JOURNEY	Pg #64
26	TODAY I'M RUNNING	Pg #67
27	LOOKING THROUGH FAITH, NOT FEAR	Pg #370
28	EAGLES	Pg #74
29	MAMA BEAR	Pg #77
30	NOT TODAY, SATAN!	Pg #81
31	DEAR JOB	Pg #83
32	WE'RE ALL A HOT MESS	Pg #85
33	MARY, DID YOU KNOW?	Pg #87
34	WHAT'S YOUR MINISTRY?	Pg #89
35	WHO'S PRAYING FOR THEM?	Pg #91
36	JESUS, BRING THE RAIN	Pg # 93
37	CLANGING CYMBAL, ANNOYING DISTRACTION	Pg #95
38	WAR STANDARD	Pg #97
39	STAY OUT OF EGYPT	Pg #99
40	I MISS MY TIME WITH YOU	Pg #101
41	A FORM OF GODLINESS	Pg #103

JESUS, FAMILY, & COFFEE

JESUS, FAMILY, & COFFEE

JESUS, FAMILY, & COFFEE

1
ARE YOU A DAHLIA, OR A SNAPDRAGON?

"He has made everything beautiful and appropriate in its time. He has also planted eternity [a sense of divine purpose] in the human heart [a mysterious longing which nothing under the sun can satisfy, except God]--yet man cannot find out (comprehend, grasp) what God has done (His overall plan) from the beginning to the end."

Ecclesiastes 3:11 AMP

I'm made beautiful in my own time. I can't bloom and blossom out of season. Just as the snapdragon blooms in winter, the lilac blooms in the spring. Likewise, a dahlia thrives best in summer, while a chrysanthemum shines in the fall. If I'm a snapdragon, I can't expect to bloom in the heat of the summer. If I'm a dahlia, I'll never bloom at my full potential in the dead of winter. We're all different, and like the many unique flowers God created, we all have different seasons.

Even though our friends may seem to be blooming while we seem to be stuck, we have to understand that it simply isn't our season. A time of not blooming doesn't mean we're dead. It means we're being prepared to bloom. The temperature has to be right. The moisture needs to be right. Our roots have to be extended deep into the ground so they are able to bear the load when we're laden with buds and blooms. It will be our turn soon enough. But getting to the place where and wen we can bloom is a process- we just have to trust it. If we aren't ready to bloom, if it's not our time, and we try to bloom out of our season, we're bound for failure. If we haven't gotten enough water (the Word, prayer, fasting) we won't be able to withstand the blooming process. We will eventually run out of water and die from thirst. If it's too hot or too cold we could freeze or dry up and wither away. The temperature (timing and atmosphere) has to be right for our blooms. If our roots aren't buried deep, with plenty of strength and muscle, we can fall. The work isn't over when we bloom. There's still a load to near, and upkeep to be done in order for our blooms to stay healthy and vibrant.

Simply put, if it's not our time, we won't survive. God has a specific time and season for each of us, and it's up to us remain patient and work fervently to ready ourselves for our season. We can't get distracted in the winter watching the snapdragons bloom, wondering wen our time will come. We must weed our lives of the bad, and water ourselves with the things of God. We should be so busy building up our root system that when the flowers around us bloom, we don't have time to question, "Why them and not me?" Likewise, we have to be joyful for those blooming around us. They've gone through their seasons of growth. We can't resent their blooming season, lest it stunt our growth and cause us to miss out on some of our own blooms. (Jealousy and bitterness **always** kill growth.)

We're all planted in this garden together. We all have seasons of growth and seasons of blooming. We can't all bloom at the same time. If we did there would be seasons of deadness, with no beauty to share with the world. We have to tend to our roots and plants while waiting on our season to bloom. It takes each of us, growing, pruning, blooming, and working together to keep the light and beauty of our God alive and breathing life into this dark world.

2
COULD I LAY MY ISAAC DOWN?

A sweet friend of mine sings a song titled, 'When I Lay My Isaac Down'. If you've never heard it, look it up. It begins by telling the story of how Abraham prayed to God for a son. God answered that prayer and gave him the greatest gift he'd ever known, a son named Isaac. Many of us know the story and know that God asked Abraham to give Isaac as a sacrifice. In the end, God provided a ram for the sacrifice, yet Abraham had still been willing to give his only son. But the part that really pricks my heart is in the chorus. It says I may have a broken heart, but my Father is proud and He didn't really want **what** I laid at the altar, He wanted **me**. Wow, right? I mean, I've read and heard this story more times than I can count but I've never seen it in this light. God doesn't just want me to be willing. He wants ME. All of me. In accomplishing that, He may need to ask me to sacrifice my 'Isaac' that I've set between me and God.

Now let me tell you the other part that got me. It hit me like a punch in the gut. My friend that sings this song? She's amazing. Strong, caring, willing, and ready to do God's will. She's also a modern day Abraham. Except God didn't provide a ram for her. She no doubt has dedicated her children back to God like so many of us have. We stand before God and our church families and we dedicate ourselves to be the best example of Christ to our children that we can be. We also dedicate our children back to Him. In essence, we give back to Him the blessings that He has given us. I can tell you as a moma to think about surrendering my children wholly to Him is scary. He created them, He trusted them to our care, but we're human and it's scary.

My friend did this, but little did she know that God was going to ask her to lay down her Isaac. Now don't confuse what I'm saying here. I don't think she was in any way punished, or had done anything wrong. I believe God had a divine plan for her, her family, and her child. She entrusted God with her baby, and just over two years ago (at the time this was written) God called her baby home to live with him. Yet during a Wednesday night singing, this moma played and sang about laying her Isaac down.

I want that faith. I want that rock solid relationship with Him; that though He doesn't provide a ram, and my Isaac is taken from me, that I still stand before Him and sing His praises. Do I think she hasn't had bumps in the road? No. She's had craters. She's had pits she's had to claw her way out of. But her foundation was rock solid. It was built on The Rock. My Isaac may not be a child God asks me to surrender to Him. It could be any number of things, or people. We all have an Isaac in our life somewhere. We're moms. We're sisters, daughters, aunts, wives, and friends. We may even be grandmothers. Mostly, we're human. We're all saved by grace and scraping through this world trying to make it to Heaven. We're trying to follow His word and His leading. We've set our eyes on Him and we're daily striving to be more like Him and do His will. We're bound to get bruised, tossed against the rocks, and beat down in this life. We may have scars, but we can be victorious. I pray that we all have the courage to not only lay our Isaacs down, but to dig deep in our faith and come out on the other side still singing His praises.

'And Abraham took the wood of the burnt offering, and laid it upon Isaac his son; and he took the fire in his hand, and a knife; and they went both of them together.'

Genesis 22:6

3
THERE ARE NO ORPHANS OF GOD

The other day I was having a conversation with a friend and she was having an off day. You know those days where you feel like you don't know your purpose in life, and you just feel so anxious because you feel like you should know, have a plan, and be working toward this goal? She was having one of those days. She looked at me and said, "I'm not like you. You KNOW what your main calling and purpose in life is." For a split second I thought, 'Huh? What is she talking about?' I mean, I'm a good 8 years older than her and I'm just starting to see and understand some of the things God is calling me to do. Then it hit me. She was talking about my kids. I'm called to be a mom. Wow. I get so lost and caught up in the day to day that I lose sight of what being a mother really is. It's a calling. It's my purpose. I feel there are other places in my life that God wants to use me. But I can't take my children lightly. I can't forget that when He blessed me with these little people, He intended for me to bloom and grow in motherhood. He intends for me to plant seeds, and grow a harvest in my children. As momas I know we get distracted by house cleaning, laundry, cooking, diapers, grocery buying trips, a continual supply of Legos in our floors, and seemingly never-ending duties that require mom and mom alone. May we always remember, though, that we are called just as sure as the teacher or nurse. Our homes are our mission fields, and our children are the souls we're touching every day. You may be a working moma, or you may be a full time mom at home. Either one is a calling, and God is looking down and smiling. I think He wants us to know, Good job, mom. Keep pushing through. I know it's hard now, but keep growing and producing fruit. You're going to reap the fruits of your labors one day in the form of your children working for His kingdom.

Now that I've gotten that piece out of the way, here's my main thought for this devotion. One Sunday evening when I got to praise team practice, the praise team leader/my friend looks at me and asks, "Hey did you like that song I sent you the other day?" I told her sure I did. (I should have known. I was hesitant but I walked right into it!) She then says, "Good! I want you to learn it to sing at the next singing!" So I start really listening to it. I'd heard it before but it had been a good while, and I needed to learn the words. The song is called 'Orphans of God' by Avalon. It's a great song. The lyrics tell us that are no orphans, strangers, or outcasts in God. That same evening I'm scrolling through my

Facebook and I see a post by a children's home I follow. Now bear with me here, because I'm tearing up. There in the middle of my newsfeed was a picture of a little boy receiving the Holy Ghost at a youth camp. The post with it told how this boy had only been at their home for a short time but heard about youth camp and wanted to go. Here's where your heart will break. While he was talking to his house father he asked him, "You are coming back to get me, right?" Be still my heart, while I pick up the shattered pieces. Now this precious little soul has Jesus living inside him, and he's not an orphan anymore and will never be alone.

Whether we have a similar story to this little boy, or we grew up in a home with both parents, a single parent, or step parents in the mix, we're not any of us orphaned or unloved. At some point in our lives we have felt or will feel alone and like we just don't fit in anywhere. That's simply not true. The Bible tells us that because of the love the Father gave us we are called the sons of God. I'm a daughter of God. He loves me that much. He doesn't see me as a misfit, an outcast, an orphan, or a square peg in a round hole. He sees me as His child. A child that He loved so much that He sent His only son to die on a cross to ensure that I would never be lonely again, and that I would one day live forever with my Father. A father who won't forsake us. He won't disappoint us, or hurt us. He won't leave us wanting for His love. He hurts with us in our hard times and He rejoices with us in our good times. What a love that is! It's a love so deep that we can't possibly comprehend it. If you're feeling lost, alone, overwhelmed, or afraid, then take heart! Jesus loves you, and you are never alone. You're not an orphan. You do fit in. You are loved. You are special. You are beautiful. You are chosen. You're a child of the King. It's up to us to not only remember that we are loved and wanted, but to ensure our precious blessings, our children, know that they are loved by us and by their Heavenly Father.

'Behold, what manner of love the Father hath bestowed upon us, that we should be called the sons of God: therefore the world knoweth us not, because it knew him not.'

1 John 3:1

4
'RISE UP' A CALL TO WOMEN WARRIORS

I have something to write here that I truly hope will lift up, encourage, and strengthen us to press on. In this chapter, I'm issuing out a challenge to myself and every lady who reads this. Every lady regardless of age, marriage status, or place in life is included. My challenge is this: Rise up!

It's time for us to rise up. Every day there is another tragedy in the news. There's confusion and heartache and pain everywhere we look. But there is hope. Our churches are experiencing revival like never before. Truly the end time revival is here. Now is not the time to slack off, be discouraged, or to lay your weapons down. It's time to rise up, my fellow women warriors, and step up to the challenge that God has placed before us. I'm not speaking just to the wives and mothers today. It's for each of us. We each have family, friends, and co-workers that need and deserve this message of hope. Furthermore, there are people that we don't know that are walking the streets in our towns and communities that are hurting and desperately need a woman warrior to touch their life. Maybe you won't directly come into contact with them, but intercessory prayer knows no bounds. We may never know who or how weve touched someone when we follow the Lord's call to hit our knees and pray.

The Bible is full of women who rose up and were used mightily by God. Take for example Deborah and Jael. Deborah was a prophetess in Israel. Judges 5:7 refers to her as a mother of Israel. Barak had been called by God to deliver the children of Israel from the hands of Sisera. Deborah told Barak that the Lord was going to deliver Sisera into the hands of a woman. Indeed, when Sisera fled, Jael called him into her tent under the guise of helping him. He met his end there at the hands of Jael. Judges 5:24 says, 'Blessed above women shall Jael the wife of Heber the Kenite be, blessed shall she be above women in the tent.' Two women with different backgrounds and stories but brought together because of their willingness to follow the call of God. Because of these women allowing themselves to be a vessel, God's people were delivered.

Ruth refused to let her mother-in-law, Naomi, travel back to Judah alone. She said, where you go I'll go, and this Ruth certainly did. She went back with somewhat bitter Naomi and was willing to work and help take care of her. She went above and beyond what she was expected to do.

She had a graceful attitude in the midst of her personal pain, she had lost her husband. In Ruth 3:11 Boaz tells her that all of the city of his people knew that she was a virtuous woman. Eventually Ruth and Boaz were married and had a son. His name was Obed, the father of Jesse. Jesse was the father of David. Do you see what I see? This is the lineage of Jesus. A woman who had been widowed, followed her mother-in-law to a strange country, she took on her God and her people, she worked in the fields, and she surely knew pain and feeling the part of the outcast. But she was graceful and courageous. She rose up when God called her, and she did so with humility. Her works were rewarded with favor.

My absolute favorite story in the Bible is the story of Esther. A small town girl turned queen and heroine to her people. After being through the purification processes, being named queen, and learning how to be queen Esther then literally put her life on the line when she went before King Ahasuerus to save her people. How far outside of her comfort zone do you suppose she was? Mordecai told her, 'Who knoweth whether thou art come to the kingdom for such a time as this?' All of Esther's people were saved from death because she stepped out of her comfort zone and rose up to the work God had placed before her. I have no doubt that if Esther had not stepped up to the plate that God could have used someone else. But He called Esther. For such a time as this. I've heard that phrase many times, and I've often used it for myself. I wonder why I was chosen to be part of this last generation that will most certainly see the coming of Jesus. I'm raising children in a world gone mad. I'm seeing and hearing and facing issues that are so far out in left field that I have to remind myself that this is the world today. For such a time as this. What if God is calling us just as He called these women? It's no accident that you and I are the women here today. I'm nothing special, but I believe that God chose our generation just as He chose the ones before us. We have a work to do just as they did. Generations of women before us have risen up and become warriors. They worked from sun up until sun down in the fields, cooking and raising children. Many times they walked or rode in buggies to get to church only to get there and sit in the heat under a tent on a hard wooden 'pew'. For such a time as this. Sometimes I feel like I can't make it from the front door to my car in this humid Louisiana heat. Yet they did it. I get flustered and my feathers get more than a little ruffled trying to wrangle 3 kids to and from church and to keep them from acting like monkeys during Service. Somehow in my mind's eye I don't see those women letting their kids deter them from getting what they came for. For such a time as this. I've heard about brush arbor services, and miracles being done and witnessed. I don't think that's over! I think it's for a time like now. I think it's time that we rise up to what we are called to be.

Women, I challenge each of us to rise up. We need to reach out to those that are hurting, hit our knees for the lost and dying, fast for the weak and lonely, and stop sitting on the power that we possess. What revival could we see if each one of us resolved to step up? How could we influence our churches, families, and communities if we laid more of our 'self' down and put more of Jesus in that place? We can't sit back and let the men do all the work. This call is to all women, but wives we have a special calling. Oftentimes I've joked with my gal pals about my husband being the head but the wives being the neck that turns the head. Yesterday it hit me that the neck supports the head. We don't control it, we support it. We need to give our husbands a support system! We need to bind together and take back our marriages, our children, and our homes. Those DO NOT belong to the devil and I refuse to allow him any space in mine. We're the keeper of our homes, and we need to embrace that and seek His face as we protect what the 4 walls of our homes contain. As I challenge you each today, I'm challenging myself. Today I determine to pray over my children more, to lift up my husband more, and to be the woman warrior that God called me to be. It's going to take sacrifice on my part. It's going to require going farther out on that proverbial limb than I've ever gone before. I'm going to have to give more of myself than I've ever given, and force this flesh into submission like never before. I may lose sleep, miss meals, and shed many tears but I want to be used. I want to be like Jesus, and I want to help further His kingdom. I want to rise up and leave a legacy for my children, and be a blessing to my husband. I want to be a woman warrior for such a time as this.

Favour is deceitful, and beauty is vain: but a woman that feareth the Lord, she shall be praised. Give her of the fruit of her hands; and let her own works praise her in the gates.

Proverbs 31:30-31

5
TAKE THESE HANDS

There's an old song that inspired this chapter. It's sung like a prayer, asking God to take these physical hands and life, and to lift them up. I've been thinking a lot about why we are here on this earth, what our mission is, and who we are here for. I think it boils down to this: We're here for the kingdom, to witness to and carry as many people as we can to Heaven, and we're here for whosoever will. The first two parts aren't always the hardest parts to fulfill, and they aren't the ones on my heart today. The part that is on my heart lies with 'whosoever will'. Have we ever thought about who is going to be hungry in this end time revival? Think about it like this, when it's supper time who's hungry? It's not my 4 year old that has been sneaking and gorging on candy and chips all afternoon. It's those of us that haven't had anything to eat, that have gone since lunch time or breakfast without anything to fill our bellies. We're empty, and we're hungry.

That, my friend, is who is coming to the Master's table now. Those that are hungry. It's not the souls that are sitting in churches having their bellies filled with candy and junk food, but the ones who are hungry for truth, love, and a real meal. More likely than not these same people aren't going to be what some might consider the best of the best. In many cases they're going to be people who have given up hope and whom others have given up hope for. Slowly our churches are drawing alcoholics, drug addicts, and convicts. Why? Why is this precious gospel drawing this crowd? Because they're hungry. Because everyone gave up on them. Because no one else can and will love them. But Jesus loves them. Oh, how Jesus loves them! So many times we forget that Jesus loves the hopelessly lost just as much as He loves us. Even the apostle Paul said in I Corinthians 15:10, "But by the grace of God I am what I am: and his grace which was bestowed upon me was not in vain; but I labored more abundantly than they all: yet not I, but the grace of God which was with me." But for the grace of God, there go I! If not for His grace how easily it could have been you or I who was lost and undone. We could be living on the streets or hopelessly addicted. We could be loveless and without hope. We could be hungry, and for more than just food.

Romans 12:9 says "Let love be without dissimulation". When I read this verse I began to wonder what the word 'dissimulation' meant. So I looked it up. It means to hide under a false appearance. Related words listed with this definition were fake, put on, sham, bluff, disguise, conceal, and impersonate. So this verse is telling me to love without being fake or impersonating love? What does that mean? I think it means to love others how Jesus loves us. When we see someone walk into our sanctuary and they don't look, talk, smell or act like we do or like we think they should, love them. Don't see their outward appearance or their circumstances as they are. Look at their soul and what Jesus can do. Look at what a testimony their life can be when God fills their heart and their life and truly love them. Love them with a love like Christ showed when He gave His life for us.

I Corinthians 13:1 says, "Though I speak with the tongues of men and of angels, and have not charity, I am become as sounding brass or a tinkling cymbal." No room for impersonation there. It doesn't matter what we say if we don't have love. Our words are empty and hollow if our actions don't back them up and have love. I'm not talking about hugging a sister or patting a young person on the back and saying, "I love you", and moving on. I'm talking about real, genuine, sacrificial love. Love that has us weeping in the altars with people we don't know. Love that has us reaching out to the lady checking us out at Wal-Mart because the Holy Ghost moved on us to do so. Love that prompts us to take food to a sick neighbor, or pray for the person that used us so wrongly last week. Love that has us helping someone that doesn't deserve it, doesn't meet the average approval of others, and doesn't meet society's level of expectation. I'm talking about real love. Love like Jesus showed us. If we are truly honest with ourselves, we know that not ONE of us deserved for Him to give His life for ours. We don't deserve the mercy He so freely gives us on a daily basis. We don't deserve the blessings that Heaven pours out on us even on our worst days. But for God's grace, there go I.

We are the body of Christ. We are His hands and feet on this earth and it is up to us to bring love and truth to His people. We've got to get His love buried in our hearts so deep that we can show it to others. To the ones that are hungry. It might not make us popular, and it may go unnoticed. We may be uncomfortable, and we may feel the unction to love someone that has been labeled a lost cause. But there are no lost causes to Jesus. There is not one person that is so messed up, caught up, or addicted that He can't break their chains of bondage and free them to a life they could only imagine. God forgive us if we turn our noses up and look away when we come in contact with them, or they come into our churches. This world has already passed them by when they were lying in the road needing help. They're looking for someone like the Samaritan that doesn't care who they are or what they've done. They're hungry for love. When Jesus told the disciples the story about the Good Samaritan He told them, "Go, and do thou likewise." That's our mission here. We need to seek out and love those that have been passed over, given up on, ignored, hated, and labeled hopeless. We need to get down to the level Jesus did. He washed His disciples feet and He was the Son of God, the Word made flesh. Yet He got down and washed their dusty, dirty feet to show us a perfect example of love and humility. If we can't do that, we can't have love. If we don't love the unlovable, who will?

It's my prayer today that He will take my hands, that they may reach down to the ones who have fallen into a place so low they can't pull themselves out on their own. I pray He takes my body, that it may be a living sacrifice for Him, broken and restored into a vessel that He can use. I pray He takes my heart, that it may be break, as His is broken, when I'm faced with the heartache this world has pressed upon the people He died to save. Lastly, I pray He takes my time on this earth, that it will be used to edify His kingdom. May it no longer be my own, but His. I pray He takes all that I am and have, and uses it for His glory.

6
REMEMBER THE LILIES

Consider the lilies how they grow: they toil not, they spin not; and yet I say unto you, that Solomon in all his glory was not arrayed like one of these. If then God so clothe the grass, which is to day in the field, and to morrow is cast into the oven; how much more will he clothe you, O ye of little faith? But rather seek ye the kingdom of God; and all these things shall be added unto you.

Luke 12:27-28, 31

These are some of my favorite verses in the Bible. Luke couldn't have captured my heart and attention better with any other analogy. Consider the lilies. To me, those three words have a musical quality to them. Birds and flowers are some of my favorite things, and they're such a representation of God's handiwork. The red birds and petunias that I favor never seem to have a care in the world. My flowers bloom wherever I plant them, with the proper care, and the birds sing their songs regardless of rain or sunshine. So when I take the time to consider the lilies, so to speak, I see a pattern. The lilies don't worry about what each day holds for them. They take each day with the assumption that their needs are going to be provided. How much worry and stress could we rid ourselves of if we remembered the lilies and applied their attitude to our lives?

Life on this earth affords us many pleasures, but it also dishes out pain and stress. I personally believe that stress, worry, and busyness are distractions put in our paths by the devil. What could make him happier than a child of God who is so distracted and weighed down that they can't even lift their heads, much less their hands in worship? In the midst of the pain and confusion life can throw at us, we have to remember that nothing surprises God. He knew I would struggle with headaches last week just as he knew my baby would be out of whack from teething this week. If He has the very hairs on our head numbered, then we surely can't doubt that He knows every detail of our lives. More importantly, He cares about them. He cares when I have a headache I can't shake, or my baby is fussy because he's trying to get a tooth. Even more so, when we're hurt or betrayed by others, He knows and cares. When the bills exceed the paycheck, He knows and cares. When we feel like life has turned us upside down and left us without any real answers or solid footing, He knows and cares. We have to remember to have faith, and keep our faith strengthened. Faith is most important when it is the most difficult to see the answers, and the storm is raging the hardest.

While I was reading an article about lilies, I read something interesting. One type of lily is said to remain open day and night, and its fragrance increases in the darkness. Despite unknown darkness, it's sweet smell gets stronger. The same is true with you and I. It's in the darkest times that we get sweeter. When we put our faith completely in God trusting that He has a plan for us and knowing that He has never failed us, we can bloom day and night. Many times we get disappointed in this life. We have to remember where our faith stands. Our faith is in the One who created the moon and stars, and told the ocean how far on the shore it could roll. Can we doubt that the God who did those things and cares even for the lilies and sparrows doesn't care for us, and won't provide for our needs? There not a storm so fierce that He can't calm it, or a need so big that He can't provide it.

God clothed the grass knowing that its purpose was to be thrown into the furnace the next day. How much more will He take care of us, the ones He died for? I feel like I can't adequately express what my heart wants to say. God sees us. He loves us. He knows our needs and circumstances, and He hasn't forgotten us. He WILL provide and carry us through whatever situation we may be facing. Finances, grief, worry, stress, hurt, sickness, and disappointment-whatever you're dealing with God knows your heart. He hears your prayers. More than anything, He loves you and He cares about you. Sometimes we have to go through the fire to come out as gold, and that's never a pleasant road to travel. But if we earnestly desire God's will in our lives, then we will go through the fire relying on God to bring us out on the other side. Whatever you're facing today, remember the lilies. The God of Heaven and Earth provided for them and He will carry you, too. Dig deep in your faith and let your fragrance grow strong and sweet in whatever darkness you find yourself in.

7
LET ME WALK WITH YOU JESUS

My son recently asked me if I loved someone, and if I did, was I praying for them. It hit me between the eyes that my 8 year old son could plainly see the connection between love and prayer. Not only my love for someone, but my love for Jesus. If I truly love Jesus, then I should be praying for my neighbor. Someone offended me? Pray for them. Someone hurt my feelings? Pray for them. Someone is talking about me, or spreading untruths? Pray for them. Someone is judging or bashing me for who I am, what I believe and stand for? Pray for them. Someone is filled with hate, judgement, and evil? Pray. For. Them. Believe me when I say I'm preaching to the choir here. Every word I type I'm saying in my heart, this is what you've got to do, Tiff. This is the only way. This is the only answer. Love and prayer are going to get us through.

Recently I have reread Romans chapter 8 several times. Each time I read it I feel like Paul is telling me exactly what I need for this day and hour. Verse 35 asks, "Who shall separate us from the love of Christ? Shall tribulation, or distress, or persecution, or famine, or nakedness, or peril, or sword?" This sounds like the world we live in to me! Nothing this world throws at us can separate us from the love of God, folks. Paul confirms in in verses 37-39, "Nay, in all these things we are more than conquerors through him that loved us. For I am persuaded that neither death, nor life, nor angels, nor principalities, nor powers, nor things present, nor things to come. Nor height, nor depth, nor any other creature, shall be able to separate us from the love of God, which is in Christ Jesus our Lord." He even says things present nor things to come. It's like he knew what we would see today, and he's saying, that can't tear you away from God's love! Tomorrow may well be worse, but whatever comes your way, it won't ever be enough to separate you from the love of God. But here's something that pricked my heart. He says, "shall be able to separate from the love of God WHICH IS IN CHRIST JESUS OUR LORD." Another verse came to me as I was reading this, so I looked it up. 1 John 4:8 says, "He that loveth not knoweth not God: for God is love." The next four verses seemed to flow off the pages. "In this was manifested the love of God toward us, because that God sent his only begotten Son into the world, that we might live through him. Herein is love, not that we loved God, but that he loved us, and sent his Son to be the propitiation for our sins. Beloved, if God so loved us, we ought also to love one another. No man hath seen God at any time. If we love one another, God dwelleth in us, and his love is perfected in us." Now, maybe you can't see the connection, and it was only something my feeble mind and heart connected. But oh, did it connect! If we can't love other people, then we can't know God. If we can't have love for others, we can't have God's love in us. Not death, nor life, nor tribulation, nor persecution can separate us from the love of God, but what I connected here was the lack of love for others can separate us from the love of God. If we can't love the very people God sent His Son to die for, how can we truly love Him? He didn't just die for me. He died for my neighbor. He died for the man that killed his neighbor just as sure as He died for me. Evil exists and this flesh causes so many to make wrong and horrible choices, but it doesn't change the fact that Jesus died for every single one of us. Was it His will for us to fall and sin and miss out on Heaven? Absolutely not. He gave us a choice, and what we do with that choice determines our eternal life. If we choose to live for Him, and follow His word and example, we make Heaven our home. So often we get caught up in events and politics and pointing fingers and casting judgement that we forget that the same blood that was shed for us was shed for the ones we're judging. Am I saying there isn't wrong and hate and consequence? No, I'm not. I'm saying that this world has enough haters and critics. This world needs Jesus. That means this world needs me and you. They need lovers of God and of man. They need less self-righteousness and more self-sacrificing.

We can't help those who don't want help. We CAN help those that do. We don't know how many hungry and hurting people we rub shoulders with every day. We may never know. We may never know until eternity what influence we had on people. It's up to us to determine if it was a good or bad influence. When I stand before my Creator on judgement day, I don't want Him to say, "Tiffany, I put this person and this person in your path. They checked you out at Wal-Mart and overheard your conversation that didn't show my love. This person was in the nursing home mopping the floor and you passed them by without a smile and word that could have changed their day. This person read your Facebook comment that showed political and racial slurs, and that forever put a blemish on the church. They weren't able to see my love in you, therefore they were never able to know my love."

Tiff needs Jesus. I need His love. I simply cannot make it one day without the love and mercy He has shown me. I've got to love like He loves me. I've got to reach out to those that don't deserve it, and show them love, because I never deserved His love. His love isn't based on a scale of what or how much we deserve. It's wide open and never ending. His love is able to heal every hurt and cross every divide. Our country is hurting. Our state is hurting. Our community is hurting. Our neighbor is hurting. I can't contribute anything good if I'm trying to find the answers in a political candidate or in anything this world can offer as a solution. I can only help when I reach out with God's love. We don't need soapboxes, opinions, or agendas. We need Jesus. We need to show them Jesus. We HAVE to show them Jesus.

An old song that I sang to my baby this morning says, 'Let me walk with you Jesus. Don't ever leave me alone. For without you I could never, no never make Heaven my home.' Today I'm going to hold my babies tighter and try harder to walk closer to Jesus. I'm going to pray for those that I may not think deserve my prayers, and I'm going to love like I've never loved before. It's going to hurt, and it won't be easy. At some point I'm going to find myself on my knees crying out to God, because I'm in confusion over circumstances and choices that were made. But I will love. I'm going to love my neighbor, and pray that God opens my heart to love them the way He loves them, the way He loves me. We can change our world with God's love. We can spark a mighty revival with love that doesn't have parameters and stipulations, color preferences, or monetary requirements. God doesn't care what color we are, what sin we're ashamed of, how much money we do or don't have, or what our status is. He sees our heart, and He loves our soul. Let me walk with you, Jesus. Let me see through your eyes. Let me love like you love. Let me change my world. Let me make a difference to a hurting heart. Let my heart break for what your heart breaks for. Let me walk with you, Jesus.

8
HE KNOWS ME

But now thus saith the Lord that created thee, O Jacob, and he that formed thee, O Israel, Fear not: for I have redeemed thee, I have called thee by thy name; thou art mine.

When thou passest through the waters, I will be with thee; and through the rivers, they shall not overflow thee: when thou walkest through the fire, thou shalt not be burned; neither shall the flame kindle upon thee.

Isaiah 43:1-2

How awesome are the words given to us in these verses? Maybe it doesn't mean much to anyone else, but it makes my heart swell to know that the God of the universe has called ME. I am His. I think these verses can be personalized for each one of us. He knows every single one of us, and we're each known to Him by name. In my mind I can imagine millions of people praying, but God knowing which voice is mine. He knows me, Tiffany Strebeck. He knows my heart, my dreams, my strengths, and my weaknesses. Yet He loved me enough to redeem me, and to call me by name, to make me His. It takes a great big God to know that many people that intimately, and it takes a great big love to make Him want to know us.

So many times I've questioned my place in the kingdom and what my 'job' was. What is my ministry, Lord? Where do I go from here? I feel like I'm not doing anything in my church, God. What is your plan for my life? Eventually I got to a place where I was almost complacent. Oh, I went to church and I hit the prayer room before service, I was still singing with the choir and praise team. (Let me insert here that I completely under appreciated the goal and purpose of a praise singer. That IS a ministry. Maybe I had my blinders on, or maybe I felt like God was calling me to do more. I was just minimal on my end, though, and that's why I got complacent. It was when I pushed and started sacrificing that I began to grow. But if God had simply called me to be a singer, and that was my part in the kingdom, that would have been more than enough. Don't underestimate yourself praise singers, you help usher in the Holy Ghost and the spirit of worship into our church services. We need you, and we appreciate you and your sacrifice!) It was when I stopped asking God questions and started seeking His will that I began to see a change. I realized that I had been trying to fit God's will into my life. My life was the proverbial round hole and His will was the square peg. I was focusing on what I thought my talents and passions were, and trying to somehow fit them into God's plan. It was when I stopped trying to figure it all out on my own that God started moving in my heart and pushing me in a different direction. I'm not much. On my own I'm nothing special, and any talent or anointing I may have comes directly from God. I'm living proof that He can take an empty, broken and unworthy vessel and use it for His glory. But He can only use me when I get to the place that I literally say, "Not my will but yours, Lord. I don't know what your will is, but use me. Mold me to be what You want me to be. I surrender all of me to be used for your glory and to further your kingdom."

God knows each one of us by name, our birth date, our past, dreams, hopes, situations, failures, weaknesses, strengths, talents, and places in life. Matthew 10:30 tells us, 'But the very hairs of your head are all numbered.' I can't make myself believe that the God who knows how many hairs are on my head doesn't see me where I am. He knows the path my feet are walking, and right after He told me in Isaiah that He knew me by name and called me His, He promised that He would be with me. He promised that the rivers would not pull me under, and that I would not be burned even when I walked through the fire. If you're walking through a fiery place right now, just keep holding on. God knows you're there, and He promised that the flames would not burn you. It may get hot, but He will bring you through. If you're questioning your place in the kingdom, and which path you should take, keep pushing. Pray one more prayer, fast one more meal, read that extra chapter in your Bible. He created you, and He HAS a plan for you, a work chosen that only you can do.

None of us were meant to just float through life with no real purpose. We're the church, and we each play a vital role. Jeremiah tells us that God knew us before we were even formed in the womb. How could we possibly believe that the Creator of us wouldn't know us? He knows I tend to be judgmental, lose my temper too easily, and get myself all bent out of shape over things that don't really matter. He knows where I'm weak. But in my weakness, He makes me strong. He uses me through my missteps, and He meets me when I've fallen from my own self reliance. He knows Tiffany, and He knows you, too. No matter what our place or calling is, God knows us and He made each of us unique. He created each of us with special abilities and talents that He will use to glorify His kingdom if we lay it down to be used. Don't get discouraged if your talent isn't the same as your brother or sister. You don't know what talent they secretly long for! Rest assured in knowing that God uniquely designed you to be exactly that, you. God knows you and He loves you. He will use you, whether His will becomes clear to you today, next week, next month, of if it takes a year or more. He has a plan and a place for each of us. He may lead you to places you never dreamed you would go and to do things that you wouldn't imagine you would do. I never in my wildest dreams thought I would be sitting here typing words from the deepest parts of my heart to share with people I will never meet. I don't know who may read this or be touched by it, but it's all for His glory. My little blog helped me to step out in faith and follow where God leads. Little did I know then that the path would lead from blog to book! There's a freedom in surrendering your will and following God down a scary, unknown path. On the flip side, we have assurance in knowing that He knows us, and promised He wouldn't leave us. Take that step out in faith today, and find comfort in the knowledge that the God who created Heaven and Earth specifically and purposely created you.

9
A WALK WORTH IMITATING

The just man walketh in his integrity: his children are blessed after him.

Proverbs 20:7

Even a child is known by his doings, whether his work be pure, and whether it be right.

Proverbs 20:11

On a Sunday night, months back, I experienced one of the greatest and most precious moments of my life. As I prayed and sought God, my husband held my hand and prayed with me and for me. We were sitting at the altar in our church, binding together in a way that we never had before. Then I felt a little hand on my shoulder, and something wiping my face. My sweet little Addison was standing there putting her hands on our shoulders and hugging us, and she had brought tissues to wipe Mommy's face with. Then her big brother Jase came over and stood in his Dad's arms, tears on his face from the presence of God he was feeling. My husband and my children sat right there at that altar and prayed with one another, and it blessed my soul like nothing else could. It also convicted it.

Since then I've had this on my heart, and now I have questions for myself. Questions like, Why did it take 9 years of marriage before Chase and I prayed together like we had? Oh, be sure we've prayed together before, but this was deeper than anything we've experienced. Have our children seen us pray like this before? Have they seen us pray together at home? When they grow up, will they know how to pray because they heard moma pray? Not just at church, but at home as well? Am I showing them how to have grace in the way that I treat others? Will they know how to love like Jesus loves, because they saw His love in my words and actions? My children live with me, eat with me, overhear my phone conversations, they see my life behind closed doors. Does what they see match up with what others see? Am I walking a walk that I want my children to imitate?

In this day and hour that we live in, I feel that one of our biggest strengths and weaknesses is our family. Satan would like nothing more than to tear our families apart and to divide our households. I think that it probably makes him quake every time he hears a moma and a daddy praying with each other, with their children, and over their children. When we bind together with our spouse in a determination to strengthen our marriage and our family units, we are putting God into a union that was divinely created by Him. What could we accomplish, and how much deeper would we and our children go if we made a conscious effort to put God in charge of our homes? If we prayed the Holy Ghost into our homes and our families? I say our family is a weakness simply because I let myself be intimidated by praying in front of my kids and my husband. Maybe it's because I care what they think, so I'm afraid they won't understand or even think I'm crazy! The past few days my heart keeps saying, 'But what if they did hear you?' I heard someone say recently that your kids should hear you praying at home. I'm trying to take that to heart. My almost 1 year old thinks mom is a jungle gym when she kneels down at her old recliner to pray, but what could be sweeter than to go to God in prayer while one of my greatest blessings is right there with me?

I feel like God is nudging me to take steps in faith, and to help my family grow deeper in Him. The greatest ministry in life that I've ever been given was the task of being a mother. How could I possibly fall short in that? How could I have stood before God and a church full of people promising to love, honor, and cherish my husband yet I slack in placing God in the center of our union? A joke around our house is that our kids gag when they see mom and dad hug or kiss. (If you know our Addison, you know this really makes her want to vomit. She says she hates kissing and true love, I'm hoping that stays for the next 20 years or so! Ha!) That never stops us from a good morning kiss, or a hug at the stove. We want our children to know what a healthy marriage looks like. They've even heard mom and dad get upset with each other, and that's ok, too. But if I really want them to see something they should imitate, shouldn't they see and hear us praying, seeking God, and reading His word?

Now isn't the time to live for God behind closed doors, nor to be ashamed of our walk with Him. However, I've got to start at home. My prayer life can't only be on fire on Sunday and Wednesday in the prayer room. The only time I tap into the Holy Ghost can't be when it's sweeping through a church service, or when I'm feeling like seeking His face. It's got to be every day, and it's got to be constant. I can't pray the constant, fervent prayers of a righteous man if my prayers are only at the church or when no one can hear. My prayer life has to be a continuing conversation with Jesus, one that my children and husband see every now and then. They'll know moma prayed for them, because they'll hear her praying for them. They'll know how to reach Jesus because they heard Moma reach Jesus. I want them to grow into a strong relationship with Jesus, because they followed the steps Mom and Dad took. I don't want them to have to guess and trip along the path of life because I was stumbling around off the straight and narrow. I want my walk with God to grow from inside of my home, and overflow into the rest of my life. I want my children to see a life worth imitating when they see mine. I'm not perfect, and I'm never going to be as long as I'm on this earth. But I can chase after the One who is perfect. I can show my kids that no matter what life throws our way, or how many times we fail, we can always run to Jesus. I can show them by living and doing it. If my heart beats for Jesus, then their hearts will beat for Jesus.

Life is hard, Moms. Motherhood is difficult and demanding. This world doesn't offer any support in furthering our children's walk with Christ. We all have days we just want to hide in the closet and eat cookies, or we feel like we've been the poorest example to our kids. Sometimes it isn't so much about the mistakes we make, as it is about our choices afterward. We all fail, fall, stumble, and make mistakes. That's ok. That's part of life. What really matters is that we keep pressing on, keep pushing back the darkness and striving for Heaven. Our kids will see that in us, and they will follow our example. They're going to walk like we walk, talk like we talk, and live how we live. Do we want them imitating the example they see in us? Encourage a mom or wife you know today! Tell her she's doing a great job, and how much you admire her. We're in this together. If this life was a race, I think it would be a relay race. We need each other in order to finish and win.

10
I KNOW WHO I AM

A few days ago I posted a photo to social media that I called my 'camp meeting' selfie. I told my friends to remember that they were beautiful in who they are, and to conquer their day as the lady that God made them. I'll admit that before I posted that picture I looked at my hair, (I was pretty excited because my poof had actually poofed that night!) I checked my teeth, my eyes, my eyebrows. Come on girls, we know we all do it! We make sure our double chin hasn't made an appearance and that everything is in its place. More often than not we go through several selfies before we decide on one that can be shown to the general public, like 300 Facebook and Instagram friends. As a general rule most of my posted selfies are done with a kid, and having 3 of them I rarely have to take a picture alone! However, this time I thought you know what, I like this picture and I'm going to post it. Then something told me that maybe other women needed to be reminded of how special they are, too. Gals, our worth isn't in our waistline, our hair-do, how in style our clothes and shoes are. These days way too much emphasis is put on things that don't really matter. Now granted, I firmly believe in a modest and holy appearance; but we aren't all the same, we aren't cookie cutter replicas, and Jesus made each of us exactly how he wants us. Lately I've found a freedom and comfort with myself that didn't come as easily as before. It took a camp meeting selfie to enlighten me to the why. I know who I am. I may not have all the answers to the questions I have in this life, and I definitely don't have a wealth of wisdom, but I know who I am. I know who I belong to, and I know when I'm having some self doubt I can turn to the One who created me and find my identity in Jesus Christ.

There's a freedom in submission to Him, and in realizing that He created me to be ME. Not only in my outward appearance, He created me as a person uniquely and perfectly. I'm not perfect on my own. I'm just weak flesh, but I'm made perfect in Him. I'm hesitant to say I have any talents, and what talents I've been blessed with are from God, but there are many talents I don't have. I don't have the same talents or personalities as anyone else. No two of us are exactly the same. Psalm 139:14-18 says, "I will praise thee; for I am fearfully and wonderfully made: marvelous are thy works; and that my soul knoweth right well. My substance was not hid from thee, when I was made in secret, and curiously wrought in the lowest parts of the earth. Thine eyes did see my substance, yet being unperfect; and in thy book all my members were written, which in continuance were fashioned, when as yet there was none of them. How precious also are thy thoughts unto me, O God! how great is the sum of them! If I should count them, they are more in number than the sand: when I awake, I am still with thee." If you want a little pick me up, just read those verses aloud. He made me! I am fearfully and wonderfully made! Wonderfully. Not haphazardly, not less than I need to be, not inadequate. The amplified Bible puts it like this, "Your eyes saw my unformed substance, and in Your book all the days of my life were written before they ever took shape, when as yet there was none of them." Not only did He form me and knit me together, He knew all my days before they even took shape. How can we doubt who we are when we have been created in such a beautiful manner? It doesn't stop there though! He knew me, He formed me, He knew my future, AND He has great and precious thoughts toward me. So great are they that they're more in sum than the sand of the sea. We all know sand is virtually innumerable. Now apply that to the precious thoughts of you by your Heavenly Father and Creator. It's more than my fleshly mind can comprehend, and it puts a spark in my spirit.

The God who created the caterpillar that transforms into the butterfly, the mighty oak tree, the waves in the ocean, the Milky Way, and Heaven and Earth created ME. He didn't put me in a mold and create me just like someone else. (Some might say He broke the mold! My poor husband!) He loved me enough to think of me, and create me uniquely for the place in His kingdom that He's prepared for me. He thinks of me, and He had my days laid out before I ever got to them. Who am I to question who I am? I'm a child of the King. More specifically, I'm a daughter with a Heavenly Father who loves me in my weakness and my brokenness. We can't find our worth or our identity in anything this world has to offer us. Be confident in who you are! We all question ourselves, especially in difficult circumstances. We feel unworthy, inadequate, and like others have so much more to offer than we do. We doubt our capabilities. We wonder if we're really following God's path for our lives, because we don't know if we really can do this thing we felt like He called us to do. Sound familiar? It does to me. It *is* me. So many times I've questioned and doubted whether something was God's plan, not because I doubted the calling. It was my own ability that made me doubt, and that in turn caused me to question if I was in His will. I'm still going to question and doubt will creep in. But today I have a confidence. Not in who I am on my own, but in who I am in Jesus. My identity is intertwined in Him, and His creation of me. On my own I'm not much. Oh, but in Jesus! In Him I am enough. Who I am isn't measured by this world's standards. Most likely I am considered less in that I don't dress, act, talk, or live the way the world sees as free. My freedom is in my hope in Jesus, and in the wonder of my creation. I know who I am. I am His.

Be confident today, lady. Read those verses aloud, and remind yourself who you are. You are enough. You are wonderfully made. He hasn't forgotten you or left you. He has a vast amount of thoughts of you, and they're all precious. You are precious to Him, and He's made you to be exactly who you are. You have been created in the image of the almighty God, and specifically for your life and the path He's leading you down. He knew your days long before we ever did, and He created you just for those days. You are beautiful. You are talented. You are precious. You are a one of a kind unique masterpiece created by THE Creator. You are His.

11
LET HELL'S GATES RATTLE

I've been told more than once that my words are an encouragement. For that I am extremely grateful and give all the praise to Jesus. The one thing that I noticed as a common factor from the ones that I got feedback from was that it helped with discouragement. Left and right it seems like discouragement is coming at us in full force. Today I'm going to attack discouragement head on. We all get discouraged, feel down, and have our low days. We're human, and that's normal. But we were NOT created to be drug down, beat down, pushed around, or lied to. And that's what exactly what the enemy does to discourage us. I don't know about you, but I'm tired of it.

Matthew 16 verse 18 says, "And I say unto thee, That thou art Peter, and upon this rock I will build my church; and the gates of hell shall not prevail against it." I'd had this verse on my heart for several days, but when I read it again something jumped out at me. Jesus looked at Peter and said, I say unto thee, That thou art Peter. Now I'm going to go out on a limb and say Peter knew his name. I don't think Jesus was necessarily reminding him of his name, so much as he was reminding him WHO he was. 1 John 4:4 tells us that we are of God, and we have overcome because greater is he that is in us than he that is in the world. So here's what I have to say to the devil's ploy of doubt and discouragement. Let hell's gates rattle. Let them shake and rumble and try to bring me down and make my stop walking down this road Jesus put me on. Let the devil try to tempt me and turn me around. More often than not if the devil can just plant a seed of doubt or discouragement in my mind, then he really doesn't have to do anything else. I cultivate that one tiny seed all on my own, and his work is done. He gets way more credit than he's due. He plants a tiny seed, I grow a garden out of it, and then want to blame it on him. Mind you, he's a wily old devil, and he's not above pulling dirty tricks on us. But I refuse to give him any more credit, one more inch, or one more moment of satisfaction over seeing me beat down with doubt and discouragement.

Let hell's gates rattle. The God that lives inside of me is greater than the god of this world who tries to drag me down. He couldn't defeat Jesus at the cross with death, and he can't defeat me here on earth because inside of me resides the very One whom death couldn't hold down! Think about that for a moment. Death couldn't stop Him, the grave couldn't hold

Him, and His spirit lives inside of me. Let hell's gates rattle! The overcomer of death promised that the gates of hell would not prevail against His church. You and I are the church. You and I are overcomers.

Revelations 1:18 says "I am he that liveth, and was dead; and, behold, I am alive for evermore, Amen; and have the keys of hell and death." Now if that doesn't make you want to shout over your coffee, I don't know what will! He lives, but was dead. He is alive forevermore. Last but not least. HE HAS THE KEYS OF HELL AND DEATH. He overcame death already, so this tells me He's going to overcome hell, also! The devil doesn't even own the keys to hell's gates! Let them rattle. Let them shake. Let them rumble, and groan, and tempt and try. You don't even own the keys to your own house devil, so don't think for one moment you're going to stop me.

I'm sick of seeing my sisters being beat down and discouraged. I'm tired of seeing the world so tricked and lied to that they think there's no way out. I'm done with thinking that my friends and family are trapped in places that seem so dark and low that even God can't save them. No more. He overcame death. He not only overcame the grave, He walked right out. He is mighty, with tens of thousands of warrior angels at His side. He created the heavens and the earth, and all that is in them. The devil himself is a fallen angel. He's fallen and wants to bring as many of us down with him as he can. Well, devil, I'm one you can't have. You also can't have my friends, my family, or my sisters who are battling discouragement. I refuse to let them go, and I've got the holder of hell's keys residing in me and standing by my side.

Lift up your head, friend. You're an overcomer. You're part of His church. It's promised that hell's gates won't prevail against us. Let them rattle, but don't let them fool you. They're locked tight because Jesus holds the keys, and He's on your side. He's given you everything you need to fight this battle, and He's preparing you to win. Speak life today. Speak encouragement. Speak peace. Speak joy. Speak victory. You will overcome. So let hell's gates rattle. They've already been defeated.

12
THE RAINBOW REMAINS

Ok, it's time for real talk ladies. The kind of real talk where I open up my heart and share with you a secret and you don't judge me for it. Are you ready? Sometimes I'm just not content, I get depressed, and I let the devil trick me into thinking I'm less than I really am. Not really a big revelation is it? Well, for me it is. Especially when yesterday I found myself down in the mouth and questioning if there was really more to me than housekeeper and human dishrag. Here's the part where you don't judge me, k? I love my little people. My kids make my heart beat and without them I truly would question myself. But every now and then, just a little bit, I wonder if that's all I am. Am I just the cereal sweeper, the clothes washer, the diaper changer, the cook, the maid, the bobo kisser, etc.? Don't confuse me here. All of those things are what I live for, and the privilege of staying home with my 3 kiddos is one I'll forever be grateful for. But there comes a time when I start to question if Tiffany is still there and if she has anything else to offer. I know you moms can relate. At least I hope you can, and I'm not the only one driving myself crazy over here. I believe that raising my kids is the greatest calling I have in my life. I could be raising song leaders or writers, preachers, musicians, prayer warriors, men and a woman of grace and truth. As in all things, though, I wonder if I get lost in what I'm doing, and if I have a real purpose, if I'm expendable, if what I'm doing really makes a difference.

You don't have to be a mom to find yourself there. Young or old, kids or no kids, married or unmarried, at some point we all find ourselves questioning, What am I doing? Is this really it? Am I ever going to accomplish anything more, or great? I'm barely keeping my head above water in life now, how could I possibly be anything more? If I can't even excel where I'm at how can I go further? I've failed in some area of my life even though I've tried my best, so maybe I'm really not worth that much. For me that area includes, I've cleaned all day and the toilet is still dirty, the kitchen floor is sticky, and my clothes aren't folded. At the end of the day my kids don't care about that, and if raising them is my calling, why should I worry when things don't go exactly like I think they should? I can't lose myself in the mundane of the day to day and expect that to define who I am and what God has called me to be. Just because we fail and stumble in life doesn't mean we have dropped 7 levels on the worthy chart. We aren't worthy in the first place. God's grace made us worthy, and His grace is what will sustain us. His ways are above our ways, and His calling in our lives is what we follow, even when we don't understand.

I let the devil slip in and whisper in my ear that I was nothing more than a glorified housekeeper. That little whisper was all it took, and I let it run away. I knew after my last blog post he would be on my case, and get on my case he did. I found myself wondering if there was more to me than where I am now. The now is what matters though. Will I ever accomplish anything outside of the home, or do more than be a mommy and a keeper of my home? I don't know, but that in itself is a huge thing and I won't take it lightly. I've been entrusted with 3 little lights that need to be kept trimmed and ready and it's my job to do that. Just like where you are is your job, and your place in life. Do I understand the things we have to go through or the low places we have to walk to get to where God wants us? I would be lying if I said I did. I don't understand any of His ways. I just know I can fall back on the assurance that they're good. His promises are solid and forever. He is never failing and always faithful. That's what gets me through the hard days, when all I can say is God just help me through.

While I was in my little self-inflicted funk yesterday, I was headed to a little get together and from out of nowhere I saw a rainbow. The sun was shining, the sky clear, and it was the biggest rainbow I've ever seen. At that moment, I remembered that God's promises are where I stand. He's good. I can hide myself in His grace and find myself in Him. I won't lie, that rainbow put a huge smile on my face. A moment later, rain began to fall. From a seemingly clear sky, out of nowhere, rain drops began to fall. I found myself thinking, how quickly life can change! One moment we're staring at the rainbow, and the next the rain comes beating down. However, my promise was still there. The rain fell, but the rainbow remained. A few moments later I turned and the rain stopped. Ahead of me I saw clear skies. Again I thought, how quickly it all can change! We never know when the rain may fall, but we have to hold on to the promises. Even when we question ourselves, our place in life, and everything happening in our lives, we have to keep holding on. It may be just a little further and one more turn before the skies clear and we break out into the blessings God has for us. Maybe this doesn't make sense to anyone other than me. I honestly had no expectation of writing about my little pity party I had yesterday. But I felt like maybe I was brought low to relate to someone else, and to learn to appreciate what I didn't before.

I'm sharing to help someone else, and to let you see that the rest of us struggle, too. Does one day mean I'm not ready to fight and keep pushing forward? Absolutely not. If anything I'm using it as a stepping stone to go higher and farther. We fall, but we get back up again. We stand on His promises. We question, but we know we find all the answers in Him even when we can't understand. On our way home last night, Addison and I saw a beautiful pink streaked sky ahead of us as we drove toward home. My girl loves a pink sky, and she had said earlier that the rainbow we saw was the prettiest one she ever saw. Keep holding on, your pretty pink sky may be just ahead.

13
I'M NOT SATISFIED

Recently I found myself thinking, wouldn't it be awesome to actually live in such an amazing place? (One other than where we reside.) Then the thought hit me, No. I'm in Louisiana for a reason. I am in the place I am in for a reason. I am in the church I am in for a reason. I am living where I am living for a reason. I've been planted where I am for this season, for such a time as this. I don't believe that God is a god of accidents or coincidence. I don't believe that He sees things like we do, and He certainly doesn't see them on the level we do or through fleshly eyes. I want to be content with where God has planted me and with what He has blessed me with. I want to bloom in this season, and see where He takes me in the next one. I want to thrive and be alive and strong in the next season.

Though I want to be content where God has planted me, I never want to be content in my walk with Him. I'm at a level with Him that I've never been before. The storms that may have knocked me overboard in the past no longer rock my boat like they used to. That's not to say that I don't face storms. I'm going to fight bigger storms, hotter fires, and harder trials as I go deeper. But I want to go deeper. I want to push harder than I've ever pushed before. Even though I've reached a higher level than I've ever been, there's a level higher still, and another and another and another. I want to see and be a part of a book of Acts church, but to do that I've got to press onward with more determination than I did yesterday. I can't see the revival and miracles the Acts church saw if I flat line in my walk with God. I can't get to a level that I'm comfortable in and make a pallet and hang out there. I've got to reach that level, take a deep breath, and reach higher for the rung above me. I believe in these end times that God is calling us to do things that we wouldn't have been able to fathom doing even a year ago. I know He is calling me to step outside of my comfort zone in a way that I wouldn't have imagined. When I step out of my box that I've got my worship, my idea of God, and my ideals in, then He leads me deeper and deeper. Speaking for myself, I think I've always had God in this pretty little package of what I thought He should and could do. I knew he had done awesome miracles in the Bible, and I knew He was more than capable of doing them now. But that little box I had wrapped God into was missing a key element: faith. I had never actually applied my faith and truly opened that box and let God out to be the Healer, Savior, and miracle worker that He is. I would venture to say that just in the past 6 months have I finally opened that box and let God out to work the way He's always wanted to. He was waiting on me to push and to apply my faith in a way I'd never applied it before. I like to think of it as 'crazy faith'. It's an open, unbridled faith that allows God to work and earnestly believes that He can do the work. When I really dug deep inside myself and let my faith grow to believe that there was NOTHING God couldn't do, it was like I blew my own mind. Honestly, my mind can't fathom the ways and things that God is going to move and do. I don't need to. I just need to apply a little crazy faith and keep climbing higher and higher.

Now am I saying that there won't be times that I fight against this life, and the things the devil throws my way? Ha! Of course not! I'm a weak fleshly vessel as much as the next person. What I AM saying is that though I may stumble, I know how to get up and brush myself off and keep going. I'm going to fall, but I'm not going to sit down and get comfortable there. I'm going to pull this weary traveler's soul up, brush off the dirt and grime of the struggle, and keep pressing toward the mark. I may not run the swiftest, and I may never be the strongest, but I will fight and through His strength I will win. I'm going to go deeper, press harder, and push Hell back more than ever before. My life depends on it. My kids depend on it. My family depends on. My friends depend on it. My community, my state, my country, and my world depend on it. They're depending on you and me to rise up the challenge of this end time and step out into a crazy faith that is constantly drawing us to another level.

A song we sing at church says, 'We won't be satisfied with anything ordinary, we won't be satisfied at all.' I'm not now, nor do I ever plan to be satisfied with anything ordinary. I serve an extraordinary God, and I won't limit Him with ordinary things. Furthermore, I'm setting my heart to never be satisfied with even the best moves and church services. I always want to have more. We've had 2 men in our church healed recently, one from cancer and one from 15 years of pain due to encephalitis. That is awesome stuff! Am I satisfied with that? No! There are more needs, more healings to come, more miracles to be seen, and more lost loved ones to be seen coming through our church doors.

On a Wednesday night recently, the lights went out at church just before it was due to start. Of course we wondered if many people would get up and leave. They didn't! They settled in their dark pews ready to have church. So we sang a couple of songs and the minister got up to speak. Eventually the lights just popped back on. The next morning over breakfast Jase says, "Moma, I think God let the lights come back on because He was amazed by what Bro. Chaney said." So I asked him, "Oh really?" He said, "Yeah. When he said he could see his sons in the church the lights came back on." Still not giving this quite the thought I needed to at this point I said, "It was about the time he said that, huh?" He firmly replied, "No, Moma. RIGHT when he said that, the lights came back on. I think God let the lights come back on because he said that." Now I've kicked myself for not catching on to what he was getting at before I did. I've also thought a lot about his faith and what could happen if I applied it to my life in such an honest, childlike way. To my 8 year-old, it wasn't too small or too big of a thing for God to turn the lights back on in response to something the minister said. To him it was as simple as he said it, God liked it, God turned the lights on. What could happen if we raised our level of expectancy to the point of a child? To the point where our imaginations were wide open to the things God could do, and we praised Him and worked for Him waiting for His response?

My expectancy level is high. My determination is in place to move higher. I won't quit and I won't stop. The devil has thrown a few kinks my way lately and in the words of a friend of mine, "He doesn't know what he's gotten himself into!" I hope these words find you ready to hit the prayer room in your church on Sunday with an expectancy you've not had before, and with a bulldog determination to push harder and higher.

14
LIFE AFTER THE COMMA

This title just impressed itself in my heart during church several services ago. I know I talk about it often, but we are truly living in the last days, and our services the past few weeks have been a testament to that fact. We've had intercessory prayer like I've never seen before. We've seen people delivered, saved, healed, freed, made whole, comforted, uplifted, strengthened, and brought out of the darkness the devil had ensnared them in. One service can literally change your life, but where do you go after that? What happens next?

I used to be lost in sin, but now I'm found in Jesus. There are two parts to that sentence, the beginning speaking of my past, my old man and the ending speaking of who I am now, my new man. What separates those? Something dramatically simple, yet amazingly complicated and beautiful. The comma. That little comma separates old from new, dark from light, bound from free. I've heard a poem recently about the dash between birth and death dates on a headstone. It was about how the dash is what really matters, how you lived in that time. Something so small, but it can make all the difference. That's how I feel about the comma. A comma is intended to separate a sentence, it's a pause. See, the thing to remember here is that a comma does not end a sentence, but rather it gives a break between the beginning and the end. So I may have started out lost in sin, but that comma gave me a pause and I can now end my sentence found and saved. So while the dash on my headstone represents my life as a whole, the comma represents a pause where I was given the chance to make a change and become a new creature. Life after the comma is what makes the difference to me. That's who I am now, and my new creature is why I will one day be able to stand before my Creator and hear Him welcome me to my eternal home.

What am I trying to say here? I'm trying to get it out of my heart and into words. My blogs never had a rough draft, they went straight from heart to WordPress. (That's how this was originally written.) My heart is trying to tell someone that your story isn't over. Your sentence hasn't ended, your book hasn't closed, and you can make a choice to go forward and change your life after your comma. I used to be bound in sin COMMA but now I'm freed from sin and guilt and shame. I used to be blind COMMA now I am healed and can see. I used to be a drug addict COMMA now I am delivered through Jesus. I used to be an alcoholic

COMMA now I am washed by His blood. I used to be lost and wandering COMMA now I'm saved by grace. I used to be in chains bound in darkness COMMA now I'm living free in the light of His mercy. I used to question my existence and if anyone loved me COMMA now I've been assured of my purpose and wrapped in His beautiful love. I used to be depressed and oppressed COMMA now I'm loosed and living in His joy and peace. I used to to search high and low in the wrong places for affirmation and companionship COMMA now I don't have to search anymore because I've found all my heart longed for in the arms of Jesus. I used to think I was worthless COMMA now I've realized my self-worth in the knowledge that He thought I was worth dying for.

The devil may have you convinced that where and who you are is all you'll ever be. That's a lie! Only God can put the period at the end of your sentence, and His mercy and grace are extended to us to give us the pause in the comma to offer us the opportunity to be freed, healed, and delivered. There's no place too low that He can't reach. There's no darkness so thick that His light can't penetrate. There's not a chain so great that He can't break it. We could never ever find ourselves in a place so bad that He can't bring us out. In the words of my pastor, we cannot exhaust the resources of God. No matter what or who you are, your comma is ready to be taken advantage of. The time is now to take your pause in your sentence of life and change your ending through His grace. Don't let the devil plant a seed of doubt in who you are now. If you've already made a new life after your comma, then you stand strong in the promises of God and the new creature you are through Him. Satan was created by the Creator and therefore has not even an ounce of power over Jesus. When God has healed or delivered you, there's not a power in Hell strong enough to undo it if we are walking close to Jesus and holding His hand. Life after the comma is what matters. It doesn't matter who we were or used to be, it's our new creature that will carry us through.

Wherever you find yourself today, before or after your comma, take heart and comfort in His word and promises. If you're before your comma and ready to make a change in your life, with all my heart I say, DO IT! Don't wait! God's mercy is everlasting and His arms are open wide, waiting for you to walk into them.

15
HIS TIMING BRINGS BEAUTY

To everything there is a season, and a time to every purpose under the heaven:

A time to be born, and a time to die; a time to plant, and a time to pluck up that which is planted;

A time to kill, and a time to heal; a time to break down, and a time to build up;

A time to weep, and a time to laugh; a time to mourn and a time to dance;

A time to cast away stones, and a time to gather stones together; a time to embrace, and a time to refrain from embracing;

A time to get, and a time to lose; a time to keep, and a time to cast away;

A time to rend, and a time to sew; a time to keep silent, and a time to speak;

A time to love, and a time to hate; a time of war, and a time of peace.

He hath made every thing beautiful in his time: also he hath set the world in their heart, so that no man can find out the work that God maketh from beginning to the end.

Ecclesiastes 3:1-8, 11

So many of my writings are written through my personal struggles, and this one is no different. Doubtless, many of us face the same struggles and trials. While they may not all be exactly the same, we're all flesh walking through a world of unknowns doing our best to trust God and hold His hand as tightly as we can. From my own personal standpoint, it seems like I'm forever coming up against the same walls and roadblocks over and over again, and I'm left wondering when I'm going to get around them for the last time and never see them coming back. Reality? Probably never. There are just some things in this life that will always be there no matter what we do or how we overcome them. Eventually there will come a time down the road when they will pop back up again. The real test is not necessarily what I come up against, but how I react to it. The last time I ran into this wall did I overcome it with stronger faith? Or did I allow it to weaken my faith to the point that I stunt any growth in my walk with God?

We're all human and flesh, so it's a given that we can't always be the strongest. Added to that, the devil loves to hit us where it hurts. (Let me insert here that it's very important to speak only positive, faith-filled things in your life. What we speak eventually is what we will allow in our lives. If we speak our weaknesses and only negativity, then gradually negativity will be our norm and the devil will jump on our weaknesses and use those against us. Speak life into your faith! Speak joy, peace, strength, grace, power, love, and growth in your life, and watch it come to pass.) Faith requires us to trust God when we can't see down the path. Oftentimes we get a word or a promise from God and instantly our faith is strengthened to a new height! We're on top of the world! Until 3 months have passed and our promise hasn't come true yet. We start wondering and we start doubting. The same storm is blowing and our boat is tossing harder than it seemed to before, and it seems the Master has fallen asleep and doesn't hear the winds and rains battering us. Recently someone told me they didn't understand why their word from God hadn't come true yet. So I asked them if God had given them a time. Had God said such and such would happen by this date, or by a set time? The answer was no. So how could they possibly think God had failed them? God's promises stand forever. His word is forever. The part we (I!) have trouble understanding is that God does not operate in time like we do. The old saying is that God's timing isn't our timing, and truer words were never spoken. There is no clock in Heaven ticking away and reminding God that He is on a schedule. There are no timers, alarms, or Google alerts going off to let God know that time has run out and He can't operate past the deadline.

What a thought, right? But it's how we think, if we are really honest with ourselves. If God doesn't move or come through for us like we think He should, when we think He should, then we feel all hope is lost and it's too late, there's nothing He can do now. I'm sure Mary and Martha felt like He was too late for their need, too. To the flesh, He was. According to their time frame, he wasn't just hours late, but days late. They even told him, "But by now Lazarus stinks!" I have to be totally transparent here and admit that there are times when I say, "Lord this stinks! How is this fair? You could have fixed this a long time ago, but You didn't, and now it stinks!". I'm a very adulty adult sometimes, ha! It may be later rather than sooner, but my faith usually catches up with me and reminds me that God never promised me when He would make a way, simply that He would.

Ecclesiastes tells us that there is a time for everything. There are also seasons. We may be going through a season of hardships and pain, but seasons only last for a little while and another one will replace it. I may be going through a time of tears, while my friend is going through a time of laughter. Her season isn't the same as mine and it's critical to remember that we all fight battles at different times. We can't compare ourselves to those around us, and we must remember that we may never know what season others are in. Just because we can't see the outward signs of their time of pain doesn't mean they aren't having one. Verse 11 has a two-fold meaning for me, one of which I had never noticed until this morning. I'll start with the more obvious but hardest to remember. 'He hath made every thing beautiful in his time: also he hath set the world in their heart, so that no man can find out the work that God maketh from the beginning to the end.' He makes every thing beautiful in HIS time. It doesn't say He makes it beautiful when we feel like we can't take anything else. It doesn't promise that just when it feels like we are ready to throw up our hands and quit that He's going to instantly make it beautiful for us. That would be too easy. Our time of dancing can't come until our time of mourning is over. We can't truly appreciate laughter and dancing if we don't shed some tears and experience some pain along the way. It also tells us that He set the world in our hearts so that 'no man can find out the work that God maketh from beginning to end.' We were never meant to understand His ways. We have the Holy Ghost and His word, and faith in the promises He left us, but we were never created to understand God and His glory or His ways.

Verse 3 tells us there is a time to kill and a time to heal, a time to break down and a time to build up. Sometimes our journey takes us to a place where there are things in our life we must kill off in order to heal again. Something must die in order for a healing to take place. I've found that many times my storms were a time of killing. I had to kill things that were holding me back and hindering me from doing the work God was calling me to do. It was painful, but a healing always took place. It's the same with breaking down and building up. You can't build up something that's already built. To build something up, we've got to break it down.

The walls we erect in certain areas of our lives must be broken down and rebuilt in order for God to use us. To be a vessel for God to mold to His likeness, a breaking down will be required at some point. But God will never fail us, and if we allow Him to break us down, our rebuilt selves will be so much stronger than what we had built ourselves, or even where God had taken us before. There's always another level to be reached in God, and growth requires breaking down and rebuilding.

The thing that jumped out at me this morning in verse 11 is the way it says, 'every thing.' "He hath made every thing beautiful in his time." It doesn't say everything, one word. It says every thing, two words. He didn't list a whole, but individuals. He makes every individual thing beautiful in His time. It may not mean the same to anyone else, but to me it says that God sees each of us and our struggles individually. He sees each and every storm, trial, heartbreak, and hurt that we go through. He promises that each of us will get His beauty, in His time, for our time and our season. I may be going through a time of pain and weeping, but I'm determined to hold on to the promise that He knows and He sees, and when it's HIS time and will, it will be made beautiful. I'll take His all-knowing wisdom and beauty over my fleshly knowledge any day. If you're going through a time of mourning, hold on because dancing is in your future, and it's sure to be beautiful when it's allowed to grow in God's hands.

16
I'M GOING FOR GOLD

Lately I've been so occupied by distractions and storms of my own that I've found it easier to lay down things that require more of me than I wanted to give. I've found it difficult to write, because it forced me to reflect on myself and acknowledge the changes I needed to be making in the midst of the storm. I thought I knew a lot about the storms of life, especially the same old ones I keep fighting. There were times it felt like my compass of life was broken and steered me straight into every storm on the horizon. I got so busy 'being in the storm' that I forgot to focus on why I was there. It never occurred to me that maybe it wasn't just life picking on me, but I was there for a reason. It certainly never dawned on me that God might have put me there. I mean, God is there to hear my prayers and save me from the storm, swoop in and save the day, deliver me from pain and suffering. That's what we think, isn't it? I'm not saying that God deliberately causes us pain, only that there are times He allows us to go through a storm for a learning process.

Job 23:10 says, "But he knoweth the way that I take: when he hath tried me, I shall come forth as gold." When he hath tried me. Those are the words I've skipped over so often lately. I want Him to know me. I want to come out as gold on the other side. I haven't really wanted Him to try me on this side, and be refined. I looked up some information on the purification process of gold, let me share what jumped out at me. One website said: "Gold is one of the heaviest metals on earth. It is an attractive metal that does not tarnish or corrode. It is a good conductor of heat and electricity. It is also soft and the most malleable and ductile of all metals. Gold is extracted from the earth and always contains other unwanted elements. Gold undergoes a purification process to remove these elements and obtain pure gold. There are two ways of refining gold. These methods are the Wohlwill process and the Miller process which result in varying levels of purity. The Miller process is rapid and simple, but it produces gold of only about 99.5 percent purity." That paragraph could make up my whole blog. I don't think it's coincidence that God chose to compare us to gold. Just as gold is taken from the earth and contains many undesirable elements, the same is true with you and me. In order to become pure, and more like Jesus, we have to withstand some fire. We have to be willing to be melted down and reshaped into His image and not our own. We have to get rid of some things in our lives that cause imperfections in order to be purified. We can't be pure gold without purification, even when it's painful to us. We could try to breeze through the process, take short cuts, and come out quicker. But we won't be 100% pure. We have to go through the whole process and undergo all the steps to reach the level of purification it takes to come out as pure gold. I've come to the realization that maybe the reason I keep fighting the same things is because I keep trying to skip steps in the process. I have to go back and start over from the beginning because I keep trying to duck out when the fire gets really hot. I don't trust God enough to form me and purify me in the heat of the process. Instead when the going gets tough, I get going and I never reach the point He intended for me to be.

Natalie Grant sings a song that is currently on my repeat playlist, called 'King of the World'. (If you haven't heard it, do yourself a favor and listen to it.) The line that gets to me the most is, 'I try to pull you down, so we are eye to eye'. The whole song gets to me but that part has just really hit home for me. How often have I tried to pull Him down to my own level? Instead of striving and being willing to make the necessary sacrifices to reach higher for His level, I've tried to drag Him down to mine. So many times I've tried to figure things out on my own, relying on my fleshly eyes and ideas to take control, forgetting that He isn't hindered by flesh, time tables, clocks, or constraints that separate me from Him. Who am I that I try to pull the Almighty down to a place that is level with humans? He is God. He is able. He is mighty. He sees all. He knows all. This storm didn't catch Him by surprise, and depending on my willingness to follow Him, He knows where my path will go. It's up to me to decide to take the 'high' road where He is, or to be content in the 'low' road that I've tried to pull Him down to. What could I learn and how could I grow if I would open my mind to the realization that He formed the earth, sun, moon, and universe with a few spoken words. The wind and seas literally obey His command. Death couldn't stop Him, and the grave couldn't hold Him. The things that would happen and the miracles that would be loosed in our lives if we wrapped our minds around this concept are unfathomable. We can't begin to comprehend the things that God longs to do for us, if we would only step up higher instead of trying to fit Him into our world and ideas.

God won't fit in a box. He doesn't belong in a box. There isn't a box big enough to contain Him! We can't see the way out of the battle we're fighting. It seems like there just isn't a way for it to break and work in our favor. Let God out of the box. When I stop trying to control the outcome of my circumstances, 8 realize that though I can't see God's hand and I don't understand His plan, He is molding me, shaping me, perfecting me. When I trust in His word and His promises and remember the same voice that calmed the sea is the same voice that has reassured me time and again, that's when I begin making some progress. That's when I begin to shine a little more like gold, and start looking a little less like undesirable earthly elements. When I reach up for Him when life seems unbearable, instead of dragging Him down to meet me, that's when I begin to grow and my likeness begins to look less like my own and more like His. I can't rush the process. It may be painful, but it's a time of learning and molding. I've got to trust the process, and the One who's holding me in His hands. You can't go wrong when you trust the One who created you. He's seeking to make us more like Him, perfect us, help us shine, bless us, increase us, and teach us how to help someone else. We may never know why we've gone through the storms and processes we've been through, and we may not know who we can help with our experiences. God always has a purpose and a reason, and mostly He always has a plan. He hasn't left us, even when we can't see Him. He hasn't forsaken us, even when we can't hear His voice. We may be in a storm that's raging so fiercely we feel like we will never make it out alive, but He will make a way out. We may be battered and torn, with bruises and bumps from all we've endured, but it's part of the process. The storm and the night won't last forever, and joy comes in the morning. We simply can't have morning until we've endured the night. We're being refined and perfected by the One who is already perfect, and loves you and I with a perfect love.

17
I'M DESPERATE FOR YOU

Our world is in trouble. Our country is a mess. Friends and families are in low and dark places. The devil knows his time is up and he is frantically trying to gather as many as he can to take with him when that trumpet sounds. Where do we stand in all of this? What does the church do in the midst of chaos and pain? How do we make it through hard times knowing harder times still are farther down the path? We get desperate.

We don't get desperate and give up or throw in the towel. Rather we get desperate for more of Jesus. We get to the point where we know that all we need, and the only thing that can carry us through, is Him. More of Him. More of His glory. More of His presence. More of His hand in our lives. More of His grace. More of His leading. More of Him opening our eyes and hearts. More of Him molding us. More of Him. This week I've had several conversations with a sweet friend of mine, and so often we have talked about how much more we need to be doing for God's kingdom and glory. This gal is a little bitty thing, but I feel so small standing in her shadow. She has such a sweet spirit and a dogged determination to live for God and see her family make it to Heaven with their shouting shoes on. She doesn't want to barely make it, she wants to bust the gates down, and she will.

I've caught myself thinking that if she needs to be doing more, how many notches do I need to step it up? We're never in a place where we're as high as He is calling us to be. There's always more, deeper, stronger, higher. Just as we can't exhaust His resources, we can't exhaust our walk with Him. Until glory, we will never be finished working for Him and Him working in us. When we get to a plateau and we feel like there's more, we know there's more, but all we can see is the storm and all we can feel is weary, what do we do then? We get desperate. We fall on our knees and on our faces, we give in to Him, we lay our burdens at His feet, and we cry out to Him. It's in those times we fully realize how far we can't go without Him. He is life. He is breath. He is water. He is bread. He is healing. He is forgiveness. He is your next mortgage payment. He is your new job. He is peace. He is love. He is financial blessing. He is the way. He is the light. He is salvation for your lost children. He is solace from the storm. He is the door that opens when previously they were all locked tight. He is the spoken word. He is the

Creator of all things. He is the Master of the winds and rains. He is Alpha and Omega. He is grace and mercy. He is God. He is our Father. He is everything. There's nothing that we need that can't be found in Him. There's no place so low that he can't find us, and there's no storm so strong that He can't lead us out. Sometimes we just have to be desperate. We have to stop trying to use our eyes to see the way, stop trying to carve the path out ourselves, and surrender to His will. We have to admit that we are in desperate need of Him, that we can't make it without Him.

It doesn't always feel good. I'll venture to say that sometimes it even hurts. It hurts to go through trial after trial and storm after storm never knowing His plan, wondering why He doesn't just speak the word and calm the stormy seas in our life. I don't understand it all. I can't pretend to. Right now I don't understand the plan He has for my family, and I can't see the way out or the path He's leading us down. I'm desperate. I'm out of options on my own. So in my desperation, I'm going to do all I know to do. I'm going to close my eyes, cinch up my faith, and hold on. I'm going to keep pushing and doing what I know is right. I'm going to keep praying, fasting, and seeking His face all while blindly holding His hand. In desperation, I'm going to bend my will to it His. Even if it hurts. Even when it's hard and I can't see or understand. We're all fighting or facing something in our lives that we can't handle on our own. Whatever the situation may be, God knows, and He can handle it. He's just waiting on us to stop trying to go at it alone and give in to Him. We never know when the next rain drop may be the last, or if the top of this mountain is just a few more feet away. When we seek more of Him, we get more of Him. More of Him is what I need, so that when my strength runs out I can tap into His strength that I've been storing up.

We've all been chosen to walk our own road for a reason. We've all been chosen to be a part of this time, this revival, this season, for a purpose. We've been put here to do a work for His kingdom. Don't give in. Don't give up. Don't back down. Get desperate. Don't let the devil convince you that this won't ever end, or that God doesn't care and has turned His back on you. He cares, and He loves us with a love that we can't fathom. Just as parents have to watch their children make choices and go through the hard parts of life and learn lessons, the same is with God. Just because He hasn't plucked us from hard parts of life doesn't mean He has left us. It means we have to rely on our faith and His promises. His faithfulness speaks for itself. You don't know who is watching us, and if we give in, they may never know Him like they could have if we had held fast. In this time when the world seems to have gone mad, the church will be a lighthouse. You and I will be the oil that keeps that light burning. We need to be desperate for Him. We need to forget about all that the world has offered us or thrown at us, and get desperate for the only One who can lead us through this barren land we are walking in.

18
I CAN'T COMPLAIN

It's amazing how things can come into perspective in an instant. The things I thought I knew, and understood, suddenly take on a whole new meaning and I see things in a totally different light. This happened to me several times in the last few weeks. We've just come out of the Thanksgiving season, and we are now entering Christmas. So often this time of year is called the season of giving, or the season of hope. Both of those things I thought I had a handle on doing and understanding. However it has become painfully obvious that I didn't have a grasp on either. Nothing completely major has happened to me, no massive revelation in a shining light, and, for some, what made me see life a little clearer isn't anything new.

It started with sponsoring a child for Christmas. The packet with the pictures and information of each child was being passed around at church one night, and I just felt like I needed to participate. After looking through the papers, one jumped out at me. She was the one and I knew it! So I set out on a mission to help this girl have a nice Christmas. My niece wanted to get on board, and we decided that between two of us we could really make her Christmas morning a nice one. Because what child (even a teenager, as our girl happens to be) doesn't deserve to wake up on Christmas with gifts just for them? Now I understand that Christmas is NOT about gifts. Frankly, the kids in these organizations that need sponsors probably understand that better than you and I do. It just all came tumbling down at me when I made the statement that I didn't want this girl to feel unloved, unimportant, or alone. Will our gifts do that for her? I don't know, but we're going to try, and we're going to send as much love and as many prayers as we can with them.

I've rambled through all that to get to this: I am blessed. Oh, praise Jesus, I am so blessed!! This last year hasn't been the easiest for my family. In fact many times its felt like we've had more bad days and hills than good days and smooth pathways. Oh, but am I blessed. I have my health. I have the health of my husband and my children. We have a warm, dry home with way more stuff in it than we need. (Almost more than it can hold!) We have a dependable vehicle to get us where we need to go. My husband has a good job. We have a host of family and friends. We have an amazing church family, pastor, and pastor's wife. Most of all, we have truth and hope of eternal life. We have comfort, and grace, and mercy. I've been given more mercy than I deserve. He's loved me beyond measure. I know I have so many blessings that I'm probably not even aware of. On those days I want more, or feel like I'm entitled to more, what do I really have to complain about? Nothing.

A simple sponsorship for a child for Christmas made me realize how blessed I am, and how I haven't even tapped into the true spirit of giving. It would take some hard thinking to remember the last time I gave sacrificially. When was the last time I gave until it hurt? How often have I looked past myself and seen the needs of others, and gave when I didn't really have to give? The widow woman didn't really have any to give, yet she did and her barrel never ran out. God's resources are never exhausted. I believe if we are giving, loving, ministering, and reaching out to others He won't let our barrel run out.

I don't have anything to complain about. He's been better to me than I could ever expect or imagine. But my job isn't done at not complaining. I've got to be His hands and feet. I've got to reach out to those in need even when it isn't easy or convenient for me. I've got to love like He loved me. Not love with conditions or exceptions. Just a real, true, no bars held love for His people. But for His grace, there go I. It could have been me needing a sponsor, or my children. I could be the one with no home for the holidays, and no way to give my children even the smallest of gifts for Christmas. So no, gifts are not what this season is about. But giving gifts to someone who otherwise wouldn't have them? That's being His hands. That's being His feet. That's showing the love of Jesus. I only wish I had done this sooner. The saying, 'It's more blessed to give than to receive' definitely applies here. I feel like I'm the one getting more out of this than this girl will.

What's the best part of this story? My niece went home and couldn't stop thinking about our girl we're sponsoring. So she took His love and decided to spread it, and got her church involved in sponsoring other children in our parish for Christmas. Love and giving overflow and continue to work when we exercise them. When we take the time to see outside of the box our world is in, then we can see so much more than we imagined. We open ourselves up to love and compassion. Without those, we're nothing and our works are in vain.

19
MARY'S SACRIFICE:
A CHRISTMAS DEVOTION

With Christmas being only a few days away there's nothing unusual about me having had Mary, the Mother of Jesus, on my mind. This year I haven't just been seeing Mary as the virgin kneeling next to the manger in my nativity scene. Lately I've been seeing her in a whole new light. Mary was chosen by God to be the Mother of the Almighty. She birthed the King of the World. How awesome and amazing is that? So often I think about the perks of being the Mother of Jesus, and I forget that as His Mother Mary made the ultimate sacrifice. Just as God sent His only Son to die, Mary birthed this little baby boy knowing that He would never truly be hers.

Imagine rocking your baby boy, looking at his face, holding his little hands, kissing his little cheeks. As a mother I can remember doing this to all of my children. 3 a.m. feedings are tiresome, but also some of the best bonding I've had, just feeding and rocking my babies. I feel confident in saying that Mary cherished every moment. Every coo and every smile went into her Mother's heart. Mothers may forget what day of the week it is or what time a school party starts, or even to brush their own teeth, but they never forget the way their children smile or how it made them feel. In my mind I can almost see her there in that stable, ignoring the bray of the donkey and the smell of the goats, and simply enjoying holding Him for the first time. I can see her kissing his skinned knee. I can see her telling him stories at bedtime and telling him to wash his hands before dinner. I can see her and Joseph cheering him on as he walks from mom to dad and the celebration they have at his first steps. I can also see her crying quietly when no one is watching, as the weight of what's to come is more than she can bear.

One of the most popular Christmas songs, and a favorite of mine, is 'Mary Did You Know?'. I think maybe she did. She knew her child had a calling higher than any, and that the fate of the world sat in those chubby little baby hands. The weight of that must have been a heavy load for a Mother. We know when we have children that they're a gift from God. We know He gives and takes away, and that His ways are not our ways. I've been spared a pain anything like Mary's heart had to endure. Many have not. It seems lately there have been more and more children in our surrounding communities being diagnosed with fatal illnesses. A friend of mine lost her child to one of those dreaded monsters. I can't imagine the toll it takes on a Mother's heart to see her child, and know their days are numbered. The gift that was given is now being taken away. I don't know why each was chosen, just as I don't know exactly what it was that set Mary apart from that the rest, causing her to be named the Mother of God. Perhaps it was an inner strength that the Father knew she possessed that would enable her to wait 33 years to see her son hanging on a cross. Maybe it was a heart that loved God so completely that she could withstand the daily trial of knowing her child's days were numbered. I can't say for sure because I don't know. Maybe when I get to Heaven the answers will become clear.

Mary had a Mother's heart. I have no doubt that with every beat of that heart and with every breath she took, she lived her life for her child. We all do. If you're reading this and you're a mother you know. You know there's nothing we wouldn't do for our children. There's not a mountain high enough or a river wide enough we wouldn't climb or cross them if needed be for our children. You also know there's no pain like the pain of seeing our child hurting. Even when we know it's for the best, or it will be short lived, or for their own good, it hurts. It's also pain almost too much to bear. Oh Mary! I know you knew! Now I need to know, Mary, how did you do it? How did you watch him grow and play knowing he was to be yours but only a small time? How did you carry him and hold him knowing one day you would see Him hanging on a tree? Did you know it would be so painful, or did it catch you unaware how deep the bond between mother and child goes? Your sweet baby boy, with no sin, was to be sacrificed for a world filled with careless sinners. When the veil rent did your heart break with it? Did your mother's heart rail out when He cried, 'It is finished.'? Oh the sacrifice that Mary made. Maybe she started out young and afraid, unsure of what was to come. But she grew, just as her child did. She grew into the Mother of Jesus. When speaking to her cousin Elisabeth she said, "My soul doth magnify the Lord, and my spirit hath rejoiced in God. For He hath regarded the low estate of his handmaiden: for, behold, from henceforth all generations shall call me blessed. For he that is mighty hath done to me great things; and holy is his name. And his mercy is on them that fear him from generation to generation. He hath showed strength and power with his arm; he hath scattreed the proud in the imagination of their hearts. He hath put down the mighty from their sears, and exalted them of low degree. He hath filled the hungry with good things; and the rich he hath sent empty away. He hath holpen his servant Israel, in remembrance of his mercy; as he spoke to our fathers, to Abraham, and to his seed forever." She had a strong heart. She had a willing spirit. Mary saw beyond the pain that she and her son would endure, and she saw the bigger picture. She knew pain was to be had, but she also knew the world was in need of a Savior. Without Mary, we could have no Jesus. She nurtured him, she loved him, she raised him, and she sacrificed him. Mary's sacrifice was the greatest sacrifice a mother will ever be asked to make. I have a whole new respect for you, Mary. Your story makes me weep as I imagine your position. Your spirit and your actions make me rise up to the calling God has placed on my life. God gave His Son. Mary gave her Son. It's time for me to give my all. Thank you, Mary, for example you've set and the sacrifice you made. Our generation still calls you blessed.

20
WHAT WOULD MY TREASURE CHEST HOLD?

For where your treasure is,
there will your heart be also.

Matthew 6:21

A short read today, just to share a thought with you that's been on my heart. We've all read and heard the words Matthew penned. 'For where your treasure is, there will your heart be also.' In fact, Luke 12:34 cites the exact same verse, word for word. I figure that means we should give it plenty of thought if the Lord saw fit to put it in the Bible twice. I know what those verses mean. I've heard them quoted. I've read them countless times. I know that where my treasures are, that's where my heart will ultimately be revealed and found. Something I haven't done until recently is mentally examine what my treasures are.

When I start sifting through my life and looking and separating what I spend the majority of my time on, I find I may not always be proud of my day to day choices of time allotment. There are days I should spend more time in prayer or in His word. There are days when I told myself I was going to check on that friend that had been on my mind and I didn't. There are days that I skimmed over my digital verse of the day rather than picking up my worn Bible and actually spending time in God's word. The list can go on and on, as I'm ridiculously far from perfect. (Just don't tell me husband, I think I've got him snowed!) What's really been weighing on me is the mental video that I've had playing through my mind. It's of me one day finding my treasure, snug in it's own chest, and opening it up. I lift the lid the see what's inside, but I never reach the end and see what my treasure chest holds. So it's left me wondering, what was in there? If I could access my treasure chest, what would it hold?

I wonder if my treasure chest would reveal what I think is my heart, or would it reveal the things I've let creep in and take the place of what really matters? Would my treasure chest reveal God's word? Would it reveal the praise team and my Bible quizzers? Would it reveal this beautiful family God has blessed me with? Would it reveal my love for people? Would it reveal God's kingdom and a life spent working to edify it? Or would it reveal books, tv, a phone, a clean home, a tablet, clothes, work, gossip, envy, and strife? What am I really laying up in my treasure chest? It's a daunting thing to peel back the layers of my day to day life and self-examine each layer to see what's hidden there. Yet it must be done. The things that hurt us the most sometimes end up being the best for us. So today I'm striving to open up a new part of me and see what treasures I've got stored up. Undoubtedly many need to be sifted through and gotten rid of. A spring cleaning of the heart, so to speak. I challenge you today to ask yourself, what would your treasure chest hold?

21
SPEAK LIFE TO YOUR DRY BONES

"So I prophesied as I was commanded: and as I prophesied, there was a noise, and behold a shaking, and the bones came together, bone to bone."

Ezekiel 37:7

A song sparked this little devotion and it's been in my heart for several weeks. It's called 'Dry Bones' by Lauren Daigle. My notes have been written for over a week. For a week, every single time I got into the truck I heard this song at least twice. (I think the Lord was trying to tell me something!) I went back to Ezekiel and I read his account of being taken to the valley of the dry bones. Even though it was a dream, or vision, I can't imagine being taken to a place like that. Could you? What if it was personalized, just for you? What if those bones were clearly meant to be the lives of your lost and dying friends and family? The bones of the calling God had on your life but, like this devotion, it was put off over and over again until it finally died? The bones of the work that was started only to be put to the side and replaced by something else? The bones of the blessings God had in store for you, but you couldn't quite sell out to Him completely? I'm not sure I could handle it. What a raw thought, of being able to see all the dry bones we have in our lives lying in a valley, waiting for life.

Ezekiel said he prophesied 'as he was commanded'. That's when the bones began to come together again. How awesome to think that there was some way that we could bring to life again our dry bones! But wait, isn't there? The God that commanded Ezekiel to prophesy to the dry bones in his vision is the same God that we serve today. God didn't change. He's still as able to raise dry bones today as He was in Ezekiel's day. Perhaps he's waiting on us to step into that valley unafraid and speak to our dry bones. The Biblical meaning of the word restore means 'to receive back more than has been lost to the point where the final outcome is greater than the original condition'. What dry bones do you have in your life that you would love to see restored? Not restored to the factory version, but restored with God's definition and better than it was in the beginning?

We find in Psalm 51:12 David is asking the Lord to restore unto him the joy of God's salvation. In Jeremiah 30:17, God promises to restore health and heal wounds. In Joel 2:25, yet another promise is made of restoration from the years the locusts and worms had eaten. What in your life has dried up and come to rest in a valley of bones? Do you have lost family that have been led off as slaves by the king of lies? Has a situation beaten you down and taken your victory? Have health problems gotten to the point where you feel you'll never be well again? Are you questioning where your place is in the kingdom, and your joy and peace of mind are dried and gone?

Speak life to those dry bones! The situations are endless. No doubt each of us are facing different struggles and while we all have a valley of dry bones, they're likely all different. What is the same is our God. The God that can raise my dry bones is the same God that can raise yours. Someone needs to read this today: Speak life to the dry bones in your life! Stop letting fear have control, gather up your courage through God, and tell those bones to rise up. Claim your family. Claim your victory. Claim your healing. Claim your finances. Claim peace. Claim joy. Claim it, sister, claim it. Name it and claim it in Jesus name then rejoice over it. God gives and God takes away. It was always His in the first place. We have dark times and we have joyful times. But that does NOT mean we will be there forever. Today I pray that someone will read this and find the strength in their faith to speak life to their dry bones. I pray there is a mighty shaking in your life and those bones begin to come together again. I pray when they are formed together, they are restored to better than they originally were. God is able, so speak life to your dry bones today.

22
THE STEADY HAND OF GOD

I was recently praying with an elder at church and she gave me a word from the Lord. It was unexpected yet completely on time and I wept with thanks for the promise I'd been given through this sweet lady. I thanked God for His faithfulness and goodness. I also found myself thanking Him for His hand upon my life and my family. Truly, without His hand upon my life I don't know where I would have ended up. I'm still a broken vessel in the Potter's hands, but without those hands I could be in a dark, desperate place. While I was thanking Him for His hand that is ever on my life, I found myself thinking about how steady His hand is. Thank you for your steady hand, I prayed. His hand is not just holding me, guiding me, and covering me, His hand is steady.

You may be wondering what I mean by His hand is 'steady'. The definition of steady is: firmly fixed, supported, or balanced; not shaking or moving: regular, even, and continuous in development, frequency, or intensity. Does this not sound like God? We all know that God is unshakable and never changing. I know that, yet the steadiness of His hand had never become apparent to me. His hand doesn't just hover weakly over me and blithely swat at the things life throws my way. His hand is steady. It never wavers, weakens, shakes, is never unstable, nor does it falter. When life dumps a truck load of misery on me and catches me totally by surprise, I falter. I stumble and I tend to need time to recover from the unexpected blow. His hand is never caught unaware by any circumstance.

My two oldest kids are both at ages where they frequently ask questions about God. At 9, my son understands more than his 5 year old sister does. She thinks 'the power of the angels' in her hair means there are angels in her hair. She says that when the sun shines through the clouds and you can see those rays piercing through, that it looks like Jesus is about to come out of the clouds. A child's view on life and God is a wonderful thing! My son on the other hand, usually asks more in depth questions. You know, the ones that make me stop and think carefully before I answer. Just a few days ago he asked me if God could see the future. Easily I replied, "Of course, Son. He sees and knows everything." He always knows what our life is going to hold, and every step that we are going to have to make. How much more peace of mind I would have if I could so easily tell myself that God sees and knows everything! I wouldn't stumble so hard on those bumps in the road if my heart was fixed on the truth of His steady hand. He has never failed me. He has never let me down. He has always been faithful. Has life been a bed of roses? Of course not! Sometimes life just downright stinks. But that doesn't mean His steady hand wasn't covering me the whole way.

God never promised me that life would be easy, only that He would walk with me along the way. A never failing God couldn't possibly have an unsteady hand that wavers. His hand covers us and leads us, never shaking or becoming unbalanced. We can always trust God to be faithful and unmoving in His support of us. This doesn't mean we aren't going to face things that make our heads spin, or bring us to our knees. Life is full of joy, but with it comes pain. The pains of life don't mean God's hand failed us or that He removed it. His hand guides us through the pains of life. I don't understand why some people seem to see enough pain to last three lifetimes, while others don't suffer as much. Unlike God, I can't see the future, as my son put it. What I do know is that from my own life as an example, God's hand is steady and good. He's faithful and righteous, always on time. He never falters or fails me, even when I'm afraid I'm drowning in life's stormy seas. Wherever He calls me, His steady hand will be with me. I need only to trust Him, and His steady hand.

23
KEEP SINGING

At our house lately, we've had an abundance of rain. Every time the puddles begin to dry up and the mud begins to harden, here comes 3 days of more rain. Life is the same way, isn't it? After one storm rolls in and we're just beginning to get our legs back underneath us, another wave of struggle rolls in and we're knocked back down again.

I've noticed something when it rains, though. Now quiet times don't come often in my house, and when they do they don't last long! In one of these rare moments, during the rain, I heard birds singing. To myself I thought: Isn't it raining outside? Sure enough the rain was coming down, yet those little birds never lost their song.

Do you see where I'm going with this now? The birds were singing in the rain. Dark clouds overhead, rain falling, thunder roaring and they were still singing. Their song wasn't any different either. They hadn't changed to a sad song to accommodate the sad state of the weather. They sounded as happy and joyous as they do on a morning that's pretty enough to drink my coffee outside in my swing.

Those little song birds made quite the impression on me. I've thought about them several times since then, especially with all the rain we've been getting. I now know that they're still singing regardless of how much rain falls. Oh, how that gives me the Holy Ghost chilly bumps! Their song doesn't change with the rain! Good or bad, happy or sad, they keep singing. How many times in my life have I lost my song because of the storm? How much joy did I miss out on because I let the rain change my song? If I had kept singing, how much easier would the struggle have been to surpass?

How often is God good? I think we can all agree that He is good ALL the time. Even in the storm, He never changes. His goodness doesn't stop because we're in the middle of a battle. His mercy hasn't ended because our life has been twisted and blown about by the winds of life's storms. Why then does our song change? How can I sing a song of praise when the sun shines and all is well, but change to a song of sadness when the clouds hang over? If God never changes, why does my song change?

I sing an old song by Don Johnson called "I Can't Complain" and the second verse talks about the days when the clouds hang low, and how much we would love to see them pass on. I want to question the rain, but I know that God has never left me. Even on the rainiest days in my life, I can't ever complain about how good God has been to me. God didn't change His tune on the days that I stumbled or rebelled. He didn't decide to stop extending His grace to me on the days that I ran from Him, or broke His heart. I'm under no illusions that I've never caused Him pain. I'm also keenly aware of how He continued to love me. Today I'll fail Him and He will continue to sing a song of love over me. Tomorrow I'll lose my temper or miss an opportunity to spend more time in prayer with Him, and He will hurt. But He will continue to love, and His song and His goodness won't change.

I want to be like the birds singing in my yard during the rain. I want to sing a song of praise and adoration for my God who is continually faithful and kind. Storms may come and winds may blow, but God never fails and He never leaves me alone. Whatever you're going through in your life, don't stop singing. You don't know how close your storm may be to ending, and a song of praise will help you dance your way out of the winds and rain.

24
I WILL NOT BE MOVED

God is in the midst of her, she shall not be moved. -Psalm 46:5

A sweet friend sent me this verse this morning. I'm blessed to have several friends that encourage me, lift me up, and pray for me on a daily basis. We need that. We need each other. So to my faithful few, thanks for being my friend! Now, back to my reason for being here. Psalm 46:10 says "God is in the midst of her; she shall not be moved: God shall help her, and that right early." The amplified version puts it like this, "God is in the midst of her, [His city] she will not be moved; God will help her when the morning dawns." I don't know if that hits home to anyone else, but for me it was like that verse was written this morning, for this day, for my life. I've said before that I write from my own experiences and places in life. I'm not going to have a pity party here and let the devil have a victory, but I can tell you that life is hard. Things that aren't big to others but are huge to my family- they're hitting us left and right. It seems like every day there's a new challenge to face and another weight to add to the yolk we carry on our backs.

Now onto the next paragraph. I'm starting a new paragraph because the hard junk of life is now behind us. That has no place in this area, because now we talk about victory. We're going to speak of joy and peace and laughter in the storm. Don't get me wrong, my circumstances are the still the same as they were five sentences ago. For the moment my circumstances haven't changed, but my perception has. I may not always have a good handle on this, and a month from now some of you may need to message me a copy of this and say, "Remember when?". For now I have my Jesus-centered glasses on. For today, I've decided to carry the load but not worry over the load. See, there's always going to be a struggle. The Bible tells us that in this world we would have trouble. To me, that means it's going to always be ready to roll in at any time. Just like a random thunderstorm here in Louisiana that can roll in from the horizon when we least expect it, as do the troubles of life. There's always going to be something. Large or small, medium or hard, it's going to happen. There. We've got that out in the open. So what do we do about it? Do I gauge my reaction on the harshness of the storm? Do I wait and see how hard it hits me before I decide how I'm going to handle it? Maybe this storm is going to hurt me more than the others, so I'm going to just sit down here and let it roll around me. If I hurt very much,

I'm not going to be able to keep going. I'm sorry if that's your storm prep, but it's wrong. Storms are going to come and go. God does not. Just because the storm is harder this time doesn't mean He left me or quit loving me. Just because the boat is rocking doesn't mean I need to slack off on my walk with God or in my pursuit of His will for me. It's quite the opposite! When the storm is raging all around us, the wind is blowing things to and fro, and the rain is slapping us in the face, that's when we need to be on our knees praying through it.

When the devil was seeking for someone to devour, God himself suggested Job. Now why do you think He did that? Certainly not because He wanted Job to hurt or suffer. I'm sure with every hurt Job experienced God felt it with him. God knew Job had the heart of a warrior. He knew that though the battle would get rough, Job would fight his way through it. Spiritually I'm sure there were times when Job was crawling along, barely moving, teeth ground in determination to keep moving, however slow the going was. God chose Job because He knew that when Job came out on the other side, he was going to be stronger, walk more confidently, and be even better prepared to keep walking the path God had planned for Him. He had plans for the good for Job, not evil, just as He does for you and me.

I don't know what God's plan for me is in this. I don't understand some things and I don't have the answers. I may never get them this side of Heaven. Nonetheless, I will press on. I didn't decide to live for God only in the good times or because I thought I was going to be a spoiled little princess who would never be touched by the hurts of life. Just the opposite, in fact. Life's hurts come regardless of my dedication to God, but walking with Him and leaning on Him make life so much more bearable. And did I mention that He loves me? He loves me through it all. If I sat down right now and refused to go on, He would still love me. He's a GOOD Father. I don't have all the experience in this world with a fleshly father, but my Heavenly Father loves me more than I can imagine, and just as my children would do anything to make their father on earth proud, I'm going to keep pushing to please my Heavenly Father. He's been so good to me, how can I possibly fail Him now?

God is within her, His city, she will not be moved. My life is a city for God. Cities need improvements, and work periodically. Right now, He's working in mine. I won't move because of the work. I'm going to keep my eyes set on Him, and His work for me and continue on. I can't afford to stop now. I've come too far. My life depends on it. My husband depends on it. My children depend on it. My neighbors and my church depend on it. My ministry depends on it. Do I know how long the work will last? No, I don't. Do I know how much more pain I have to endure before the work is done? No, I don't. Do I know where my family and my ministry will be when the work is over? No, I can't even imagine where this will take us! I won't be moved. I won't give up. I won't back down. I will pray more. I will fast more. I will seek out a sister who is going through a storm and I will bind with her. The storm may not be all about me. Maybe it's teaching me to love others, to be more in tune with their needs and struggles. Maybe the work is trying to break my will to mold to His own will for me. Maybe the things that are breaking in my life are going to be rebuilt to make me a better wife and mother. Maybe when those things are broken down I will find the remains of the altars I've built in my life, but let them grow cold from misuse and neglect. No, I won't move. I won't waver from this. I won't worry over the load I carry. God didn't stop loving me and His faithfulness hasn't ended with the last weight that was set upon me. I may or have all I think I want in this life, but never failed to provide what I needed. Everything I've ever had was given to me out of His goodness, and He gives and takes away. If He has taken away something, maybe I didn't need it. Maybe He needed it more than I did. Maybe I just don't know the answers because I can't see the whole plan the way He can.

So do I have troubles? I have many. Do they try to bring me down? It's a fight every day to keep the devil's lying voice out of my ear. In fact if history repeats itself, after I hit the publish button on this blog post, in a day or two another hit will come. The devil doesn't like it when we get the spirit of Job and prove him wrong with our unwillingness to move despite his attempts to derail us. So no, I won't move. I won't stop. If I have to crawl through, dig out, break my nails, dirty my face, and sacrifice more of myself than I thought I had to give, I won't give up. God is in the midst of me, He won't leave me. The last line says He will help me when the morning dawns. I don't know how long it will be before morning comes, but I know I've got a promise that it WILL come. God gave me a promise a few months ago that He was going to do a work in my life similar to the work He did for Job. I've always focused on the blessing portion of that promise, but I have to remember what Job went through before His blessing came. I can't compare myself in stature to the mighty man that Job was, but I can take after his example and never give up or back down. I may have more work to be done before the weight is lifted. I won't move. There may be more dark days ahead. I won't move. The storm may hit again, when I think I'm at my lowest. I won't move. God is within me. I cannot and will not be moved.

25
THE FORGOTTEN PART OF JOB'S JOURNEY

I've had several ideas rolling through my head the last few days. Every time I was convinced I knew which one to write, something changed. My heart finally fell on this one, and it will be very close to my heart. I'm going to share with you part of where I am right now, and pray it touches someone who is reading this. Several months back an elder from church was praying with me and gave me a word. I think I mentioned it previously, but I never said what it was. I never would have thought to share it with the world, until God slowly began to shift my thinking and show me there was more to what she told me than I thought. Here's the gist of what she said to me: "God is getting ready to lift what has been on your family and your finances. What God did for Job, He's going to do for you, and in some way you're going to know it was Him."

Now, at the time and for a while after all I could think was that the battle would soon be over. Life had been hard and had been whipping my family back and forth. What God did for Job He's going to do for me. How could I doubt after a word like that? I had a promise from God that He was going to lift the things that had been pushing my family down. When the winds would blow us harder, I would take it in stride knowing I had a promise from God that it would be over eventually. At some point down the road I was going to see daylight at the end of the tunnel. I can't lie, at times I was walking on cloud nine. Just keep on dancing, devil, I've got a word from the Lord! How quickly I had forgotten that Job made a very long, very hard journey before he found the relief he had sought so desperately.

When my sister told me what she did, I focused entirely on the end of Job's journey. Job had hard times and he stood firm in his walk with God and was given more than he had when his troubles began. I've had troubles and now it won't be long until it's all going to be lifted if I just stay my course. How quickly I dismissed the extent of Job's 'troubles'. Job didn't just lose his job. He didn't just find himself living paycheck to paycheck. He didn't only find himself facing sick children and loss of things. He lost everything. Even his wife began to mock him. All he had left was the breath in his body and God. How quick I was to compare my situation to Job's. I wanted his outcome, but I hadn't considered that to actually get there I had to walk the first part of his journey, which was a little longer than what I had already gone.

Let me start this section by saying I still am nowhere near the circumstances Job found himself in. Frankly, as much as I know God is mighty and able, I don't know if I could have reacted nearly as faithfully as he did. What I do want you to understand, is that I forgot that to reach victory, I've got to have something to overcome. In order to reach the top of a higher mountain, I've got to climb up the rough side. A tougher climb yields a higher height at the end of my journey. In the last several months I've experienced doubt, a negative balance in my bank account, more doubt, broken home appliances, a little more doubt, truck tires that need replacing along with some shaky faith, and most recently I've experienced fear over the outcome of medical test results. I still have more tests to go through, although my praise report is that my last little test came back better than fear told me it would! I also will be experiencing taking my baby to have the tubes in his ears replaced. For a Moma, even a small procedure is cause for concern. Life has thrown one thing after another at me and my family lately. No, they're not major. No, they're nowhere near what Job experienced. But unfortunately for us, the devil is good at his job and he knows how to land a punch. A little one here, another small one there and eventually you're sore all over so no matter what he throws at you, it feels worse than it really is.

Are my troubles going to disappear tomorrow? No, sadly they're not. Will God miraculously lift them and turn them around? I don't know. He's more than able, but I don't know what His plan is for me. I don't what what His plan for family is in this struggle. Maybe we have more to go through than where we've been. Do I want to go through the pain? No! Do I want to keep getting hit left and right by the annoying things in life that break and go wrong? No! In fact, my dishwasher started making an awful noise last night and I don't know if we can salvage it or if it may blow up in a puff of smoke later. The way life has been lately, smoke is going to be in my future! Ha! I don't want to climb up the rough side of the mountain, but I do want to reach that upper level it leads to. My Pastor told a story a while back that my father-in-law likes and brought back to memory not long ago. A young man came to an elder and wanted his mantle to be set upon him. He wanted the anointing the elder had, and to be at the level he was. The elder asked him if he really wanted it and when the young man replied yes he said, "Ok then. Lord I pray you will send a heart attack.." before the elder could finish the young man promptly stopped him, clearly confused and wanted to know what he was doing! The elder told him he had not reached the place he was without troubles and trials, and indeed had suffered a serious heart attack in the years before. The moral of the story is that we all want the anointing and the mantle, but very seldom are we willing to walk the road the mantle requires.

Maybe this won't touch anyone else, quite like it's touched me. Maybe no one else is walking a road that resembles mine. However, my heart sure thanks me for getting it out there. Fear and doubt have invaded my mind enough, and I never ever want to look up the path and see only what fear allows me to see. I want to look through faith and not through fear. I don't want to forget the path Bro. Job walked before he came out on the other side victorious. I don't want to let my mind continue to think that life is picking on me, or that life will always be pain. I may never be rich and I may never have good health again but I will always have faith. Money can't buy my mansion in Heaven, and sickness can't keep me out! So I may be poor, sick, broke down, the least of these but I will hold fast to faith, joy, peace, and hope! God has never failed me before and He's never left my side. He didn't promise me that life would be easy, but He gave me hope that help would always come on time. So if my dishwasher explodes, I'll try to pray more and add more fasting to my week. If it works, I'll shout glory down in my kitchen and fast anyway. If the test results come back negative, I'll fall into the arms of God Almighty. If they come back in my favor, I'll do a victory dance and pray more anyway. I want that mantle. I want that anointing. I want to be in the place that God is trying to get me to. I've stumbled and I've scraped my knees lately. Next time, I need to stay there a little longer and use my knees what they were intended for. If I fall 7 times, I plan to get back up 8 times. I'm not perfect, nowhere close. I'm barely worthy of scrubbing the toilets in God's house, but He's decided to use me. He's trying to make me into something here like he did Job, so I'll keep struggling. I'll keep falling and rising and disappointing the devil every time I get back on my feet. I'll do my best to never forget Job's entire journey, and remember that I was created for such a time as this.

26
TODAY I'M RUNNING

I've got to be honest with you all when I say that this was originally going to be a little post on my Facebook page. Proverbs 18:10 was my verse of the day and it was just so right for me this morning. I was feeling a little I overwhelmed when I finally got to sit down with my coffee and open my Bible app. I almost felt like someone who was thirsty for a cold drink of water, as I thought, Ok Lord what is my verse today?? It was so perfect I decided to hop over to Pinterest for a pretty picture to share so I could write a few words to go along with it. (Thank you to all of the crafty people out there who make those pretty pictures for non-crafty people like me to share.) I had just hit Facebook when something inside me said, There's not going to be enough space there, you know your words are going to flow out and they're never going to fit there. So here we are, with another writing of my thoughts and feelings.

"The name of the Lord is a strong tower: the righteous runneth into it, and is safe."

Proverbs 18:10 KJV

This was my verse of the day for today. As soon as I read this, all I could think was how today I'm running toward that strong tower. When life has pushed me, pulled me, and chased after me to drag me down, I'm running toward that strong tower. God has equipped me with everything I need to run this race, but there are times that I need His reassurance. I need to feel the strength of the Almighty and be reminded of who holds my tomorrow. Maybe I'm the only weak person who's ever felt like they just needed Daddy God's arms wrapped around them. If I am, that's ok. I'm still going to ask Him to wrap me up and hold me. This morning my daughter fell off her bike and bumped her knees. There wasn't any bleeding to speak of, no cuts or gashes, but when I offered that purple band-aid to her, it just made her feel better. Sometimes I just need God to give me a band-aid when life has pushed me down again. Just like my little girl, most likely my feelings are hurt more than my knees but a band-aid from the One who loves me always gives me comfort and I'm ready to face it all again.

So today I'm running fast and hard toward that strong tower. Nothing significant has happened. I haven't had a major upset in my life. I'm not fighting anything new. For that matter, I'm not fighting anything that plenty of others aren't fighting themselves. In fact, I feel confident in saying that some of the people reading these words are fighting these same battles. Those battles the devil likes to throw in our path to try and wear us down. He would like nothing better than to catch us in a weak moment and con us into giving up. The joke is on him though! For every time he pushes me, that's just a little bit closer I get to the strong tower. I'm going to run to it and gather my strength. I'm going to thirst after Bible verses every day, knowing that the Word of God always holds something applicable to my life, in every situation. I'm going to fast even when I really want to go eat everything in my pantry. I'm going to get up and go to church in the morning, even though staying in bed and drinking coffee sounds tempting. Because I'm running.

I'm not an agile person. I'm absolutely, definitely NOT a runner. I joke quite often that my spiritual person runs, but my physical one just doesn't. Some people aren't made for running, and I'm one of them. I'm more of a possum person, you know, lay down and play dead. That's my physical body. My spiritual self wants to run. Oh, does it run! It runs without abandon toward the tower of strength. I'm going to be honest again and say that I googled that phrase to be sure I was wording it correctly, and to read the exact definition of it. The phrase 'with abandon' means: a complete surrender to natural impulses without restraint or moderation; freedom from inhibition or conventionality: to dance with reckless abandon. I don't know if that does anything for you, but it stirs my spirit. That's what I feel like today. I feel like I'm running with abandon toward the strong tower. I don't care what anyone thinks of me, I don't care if I'm cool or if I fit in with the crowd. Tiffany needs to get to the strong tower so Tiffany is going to throw restraint out the window. Anything and everything that tries to convince me that I shouldn't run toward Him is being tossed to the side. If I can just get to Him, if I can just make it into His presence I know I'll be able to keep going.

I don't know if this all makes sense to anyone. I don't know if you can follow it. I just want you to know that today I'm running. I'm running with abandon toward that strong tower. Before the day is over I'm most likely going to fall and require a purple band-aid or two. Just as my determined little girl limped right back out to her bike, I'll get right back onto the path toward the strong tower. I'm going to run toward His strength, regardless if it's cool or if my friends are doing it. I'm going to run with abandon, because I can't make it without Him. Just as a runner in a marathon may need a moment's rest to catch their breath and get a drink of water, so do I. I need to sit at His feet and draw strength from Him. Without restraint, without anything holding me back, I'm running.

I'm going to end this with a question for every person who reads it: Want to run with me?

27
LOOKING THROUGH FAITH, NOT FEAR

I'm a contact wearer. I absolutely must have them to be able to see anything. Like many other contact wearers, I wear my glasses at night and when I first wake up in the mornings. My sight is pretty bad, so one or the other are required for me to do more than stumble around my house! To give my husband a more accurate idea of how blurry my sight was without my glasses, I once took them off while we were going down a backroad near our home. The sides of the road were just lined with pine trees, along with a power line and its poles at intervals. I took my glasses off and said, "Babe, I can't even tell what's trees and what's light poles. It's all blurry and even when I squint my eyes and strain, I can't really make them out." Naturally he was appalled and proceeded to make fun, ha! Without the correct lenses, I couldn't focus on things that were important, like light poles when I'm driving. Lack of my corrective lenses will cause me to stumble and bump into things much more often than when I am wearing them. Things that I'm familiar with like the doorways and the end of my bed will become blurry and cause me pain when I stub my toe on them because I can't see. Let me just insert here that unless I am wearing the lenses that have been prescribed to me that are designed specifically for me, they won't do me any good.

The same can be said for my faith. When I'm not looking through faith, I lose focus on what's important. I can't see the things I really need to see, if I'm looking at my situation through fear instead of faith. Looking through fear all I can see are the bills coming in, rather than God's track record of always providing my family's every need. Fear only allows me to see what I'm lacking, rather than all I've been given. Fear doesn't show me grace, the faithfulness of God, or the miraculous works that He has already done in my life. Fear doesn't want me to remember when God healed my newborn, how He has blessed my husband with the right job over and over again, or how my family has always had food, clothing, and shelter. Fear only wants me to see the magnitude of the situation. When I look through fear, everything is distorted and I forget that the mountain isn't really as big as it looks, but fear has blurred my vision and it seems impossibly high. Fear does it best to keep me blinded to the things I'm supposed to be focused on.

Some things in life are a given. Life will be hard. Times will be tough. I know that. I know it just like I know that when I get out of bed every morning I can take a right at the foot of the bed, walk 5 steps and there is the door to the bathroom, then three more steps will get me to my toothbrush. It never changes. The door doesn't move 3 inches in the night. My bed frame won't get 6 inches longer while I sleep. All of that sounds simple and like a given, especially since they're part of my life. Part of my routine is brushing my teeth first thing. (I can't have my morning breath ruining my coffee!) Oh but if I ever try to accomplish this without my glasses. I'm wobbly and I stumble. I have to hold my hands out to keep from ripping a toe off on the bed, or hitting my head with the door. (Yes, that has really happened.) Life works the same way. I know life will be hard. I know the devil will fight me and my family every chance he gets. I know it's not going to be all sunshine and roses. Those things are just as assured as the location of my bed is. They should be easy to circumnavigate. Until I'm not wearing my lenses. When I start looking through fear and stop looking through faith, things that I knew were there will start tripping me up. When I don't keep my faith on my eyes, finances, stress, relationships, jobs, parenting difficulties, etc begin causing me to stumble. I get wobbly and disoriented. I can't see clearly where I need to go because fear has blurred my vision. I absolutely must look through faith at all times, or I will end up causing my soul pain, just as I do my toes when I neglect to wear my glasses.

Simple routine tasks become hard and overwhelming when I'm not wearing my glasses. I can't fix my hair, pour a cup of coffee without spilling it, or even pick up my house if I'm not looking through my corrective eyewear. Have you ever noticed that when the devil is working overtime to bring you down with fear and anxiety that it begins to get harder and harder to pray and read your Bible? Simple parts of life that were once second nature and joyful, like making a cup of coffee or spending time with the Father, become tedious tasks when we're not looking through the right lenses. My fleshly eyes aren't meant to be blurry, so I wear my contacts. My spiritual eyes aren't meant to be blurry, so I wear my faith.

My sister-in-law and I often shop in each other's closet. We wear the same size clothes and the same size shoes. At any given time we will both have clothes that belong to the other one in our closets. It just so happens that we both wear contacts, too. But though our clothes can be interchanged, our contacts cannot. Her prescription isn't strong enough to correct my eyesight, and mine is too strong for hers. If we were to swap our contact lenses the way we do shoes, we would both still have blurry vision and most likely a headache to go with it. I wasn't meant to see through her lenses, nor her through mine. Can you see where I'm going with this? I cannot compare myself to others. I feel like I need to say that again, for myself and for someone reading this. I CANNOT compare myself to others. I can't look through their lenses and see clearly. Their eyesight isn't what mine is, and it will only blur my vision. My lenses are catered to me and my specific needs. The same is true in my walk with God. I can't look at what others have, or their blessings, and wonder why I don't have what they have. I can't see their struggles. I can't see their pain or heartaches. My lenses are meant for my eyes, and they correct my vision to see what I'm supposed to see. My faith keeps my focus on what God has done for me, and how He has never failed me and will always bring me through. Faith keeps my eyesight clear and focused on God and His loving kindness toward me.

When I look through faith, the mountain isn't so scary. I can stand and say, "Move!" and watch that mountain jump out of my way. When I look through faith, it's easy to keep my focus on all God has done, and not question the whys or hows. When I'm looking through faith, I don't find it hard to read my Bible, pray, or fast. It's only when I look through fear that I begin to slip. Fear only enhances my worry and my doubt. Fear will never make my path clearer, it only serves to skew my vision and cause me to stumble around and miss the marks of the path. Fear won't guide me back to my course, only faith will do that. Only faith will allow me to continue on with confidence that everything will be alright. Only faith will keep my mind and heart at peace knowing that the righteous have never been forsaken, nor His seed begging for bread. Fear is a tool the devil uses to get me off course. If he can get me to look through fear and stop looking through faith, he knows I will fall. He knows that I will stub my toe and cause myself pain. He knows that fear keeps me from seeing important things in my life. Fear will paralyze me and blur every part of my life until I question everything. "What if this happens, God? What will you do then? How are we going to make it through this, God? Why can't you just end this? Why do they have it so easy and we seem to always struggle?" That's not faith! That's fear! Fear keeps your focus on the unknown, not the God who knows. Fear keeps you questioning everything because everything looks blurry. Faith puts everything into focus. Faith says God has never failed me. Faith says I will not fear, for God is my Shepherd. Faith says I may not have it all by worldly standards, but I've got Jesus. Faith says I don't really have any answer for how or when, but I know a God who does. Faith says there's only a little floor left in the pot, but I'll make the prophet a cake. Faith says the people are big, the walls bigger, but the fruits of the land are exponential. Faith says tomorrow is unknown, but my God is known.

Today I'm looking through my faith, and no longer through fear. I've let fear rule my vision for far too long, and in turn the devil thinks he's won. Faith has no place for fear. **I've** got no place for fear. No longer will I look at my situation through fear. I'm going to look at it through faith. I'm going to see my brothers and sisters through faith. He did it for them, He's going to do it for me! He did it before, He'll do it again! He will not fail me! He is faithful to me! He is bigger than this mountain! Move mountain! His grace is sufficient! His love is endless! His abilities are matchless! His vision is perfect. Today I'm going to take rule over fear and look through faith. Today I claim my life and my future in Jesus name. Today I claim my victory and my peace in Jesus name. I claim my family and our place in the kingdom in Jesus name. I'm looking through faith and not fear. Join with me?

28
EAGLES

The McGruders sing a song called 'From Heaven's Point of View', and I've always loved it. It talks about soaring like an eagle and seeing life through Heaven's point of view. The past few days it has really been on my mind and resonating in my heart. So often we look at our circumstances from our view. We can only see a flatlined version of what we're going through. We aren't able to see the entire situation from a higher point of view, and certainly we can't see it from God's point of view. I talked before about looking through faith and not fear. When we look at our circumstances from Heaven's point of view, that's looking through faith. We have to allow our faith to bring us up to that level, where we see things the way God sees them, to the place where nothing is impossible, because with God ALL things are possible. His word tells us that, and He's not a God that can lie. When we stop allowing fear to control our vision, we stop seeing the impossible and start seeing the possible.

After listening to the one and only, most anointed, Priscilla McGruder sing this song several times, I began to think about eagles. The Bible mentions them many times, and Isaiah 40:31 even tells us that if we wait on God, that we will mount up with wings like eagles. So, being how my thought process works, I started wondering WHAT was so specific to the eagles that this comparison was made. Naturally, I turned to Google. Ladies and gents, let me share what I found. I say a lot that this may not help anyone other than me, but just put your spiritual goggles on for a second and let's look at a few of the facts I found about eagles.

Eagles generally roost and nest in high places. Isn't that something? That one almost speaks for itself. Eagles don't roost low on the ground, at eye level. They build their nests up high, above the rest of the animals. Maybe it's just my way of thinking, but if you're up that high it would be awful hard for a predator or enemy to sneak up on you without being seen. You're in the perfect position to be aware of anything coming against you. Let me dig this hole just a little deeper when I say that if you're building your nest up high, you're separated from everything else. You're not at risk of falling into many snares that a nest built on the ground would be. Are your spiritual goggles on, can you see where I'm digging this hole? Though we were certainly never meant to be stuck up or elevate ourselves above other people, because we are all sinners saved by grace, we absolutely are called to be separated. We aren't meant to blend in with the world. When we try to rub shoulders with what we weren't meant to be like, we begin to fall prey to predators that we would have been more aware of if we built our nest in a higher place.

Eagles hold the record for the largest load known to have been carried by a flying bird. Though they don't do it often, eagles can carry a massive load. The record was for a 15 pound mule deer fawn. Can you imagine that sight, an eagle soaring with such a load? They're set apart in their ability to handle such a load. They have the strength and endurance to carry heavy loads when it's necessary. Just like we are endowed with strength through Jesus Christ to maneuver the loads we have in this life. Such a heavy load may not always be required of us, and some may carry burdens heavier than others, but one thing remains the same: we have what it takes to carry the load whatever distance is required of us.

Male and female eagles don't differ much but they are unusual in that the females are the larger, by about a quarter as much. I'm absolutely not man bashing here, I have a man that I love with all my heart! But we all know that men and women function differently. We handle situations in different ways, and many times a burden may fall on us that may not fall on our husbands. This portion is geared more toward wives and moms, I think. As wives and mothers we are the keepers of our homes, and that lends a special burden to us. We have to be built just a little bit larger so we can bear the weight of our homes, families, and children. It takes a special heart to fulfil those roles, and God certainly didn't leave us ill-equipped. He created us with a heart to love that much, and shoulders sturdy enough to carry those burdens. He didn't just toss us into those roles unprepared, but rather He specifically created us with what we needed to be the women He's calling us to be.

Eagles have confidence. They don't look over their shoulder checking for predators like other birds do. I think this might be my favorite thing that I read about eagles. One place even said it like this: "Presumably nothing is daft enough to consider the idea of having an eagle for dinner!" What if we, as children of the King, got that mindset? If we had all the confidence in the world that our Father had us in His hands. That no matter where we are, He has never left us or forsaken us. What if we girded ourselves in the armor of God, and flew with confidence in the face of the adversary? I want to be that eagle. I want to be the Moma Eagle that if the devil is crazy enough to pick a fight with me, then he's prepared to get his eyes blacked and his tail whipped! We don't have to look over our shoulder in fear of what's behind us or what may try to take us down. We have the Master of the wind and rain on our side, and our steps are ordered by Him.

I don't know what every person reading this is facing, but it's safe to say that most everyone is facing one battle or another. There are situations in your life that need a change. There are areas that fear is in control and faith needs to take over. There are decisions that you're wrestling with that scare you because you can't see the next step. Jobs are tedious. Bills are high. Bodies are sick. Minds are tired. Faith is low. Storms are raging. Fear is rampant. But my God is in control. Fear will never allow you to see from Heaven's point of view. Eagles soar higher, with more power and confidence than any other bird, and that's why I think we're compared to them so often. That's why the verse 31 in Isaiah 40 uses 'rising up like an eagles' as an encouragement, because eagles don't fear what may come. They just soar with boldness in the face of whatever circumstance they may come against. They build high, and carry heavy, all without restraint or with uncertainty. On my own, I could never dream of being those things. Confident. Able. Enough. Fearless. Strong. Mighty. Warrior. When I align myself with Almighty God, and place my fears and my very life in His hands, that's when I'm able to soar above what I'm facing in this life and see things from Heaven's view. I begin to peel off the scales of the impossible and see through the possible. Wherever your life finds you today, reach down deep inside and pull out that eagle waiting to soar. Spread your wings in confidence of the Lord, and let Him take you to heights you never dreamed of before. Heaven's point of view offers a view more grand than anything we could ever see, and holds the answers to so many of your questions. Stop looking through fear, and look through faith, from Heaven's point of view.

"But they that wait upon the Lord shall renew their strength; they shall mount up with wings as eagles; they shall run, and not be weary; and they shall walk, and not faint."
Isaiah 40:31 KJV

29
MAMA BEAR

I've been tossing and rolling around blog ideas for days. I just couldn't seem to settle on one. It's funny how the smallest, most insignificant thing can instantly inspire a blog post. I love how God works! I was talking to a friend this morning, and we were talking about praying over our homes and our families, our marriages and children. I said I had recently prayed over my home, and I refused to let Hell come in and try to take away joy and peace, and to sow discord in their place. My friend said, "Mama Bear ain't playin!". Boy howdy! That did something to me! Not only that someone would recognize this fire inside of me, but it was such a huge reminder of what a large portion of my responsibilities are: my children. My home. My husband.

Recently the Lord has been working in me, turning my heart and helping me focus on family, marriage, and being a mom. He's been ushering me to reach out to my fellow moms and wives. Clearly this won't speak to every woman out there, but I know there are some Momas that are walking along the same path that I am. Daily we muddle through our chores and tasks the best that we can, often getting sidetracked or benched by one hiccup or another. Just today I started this blog hours ago, and distraction pulled me away. I'm currently sitting here writing and drinking coffee, all while knowing I have enough things to do I could keep busy until bedtime! Isn't that just like the enemy, though? To use my ministry in my home as a distraction for my other ministries, for my prayer life, my Bible reading? Or even a distraction from my ministry-in-home against itself?

Let's face it, this is a ministry. You're asking how, right? How could folding socks, wiping noses, paying bills, cooking supper, or mopping the floor possibly be considered a ministry? Well, what else does a ministry do than to help you serve others? Family and marriage are ordained of God. I believe family units are some of the most powerful forces against hell that we have, and because of that, they are also the most fought against. When I cook supper, I'm serving my husband. I'm being the helpmeet that I was intended to be for him. When I fill his coffee cup, or greet him with a smile and a kiss after a day of work, I'm supporting him and loving him, the way God intended for me to. When I mop that chocolate milk off the floor, wipe that runny nose for thousandth time, or call out spelling words, I'm serving my children. I'm ministering to them by showing them how to mother, by showing them to work diligently and with all your might where you are put. To bloom where you're planted, so to speak. I'm becoming a living example of God's word.

But there is so much more to our ministry as women than just what our fleshly hands can do. We have to apply our spiritual hands and put them on our families. I heard it said once that women are 'The Keepers of the Home'. I've never forgotten that. What a powerful thought! My home is my domain. I'm not talking about this in terms of a woman's place is in the kitchen, or you have to be a stay home Mom for this to apply, and you certainly don't have to be Pinterest-perfect either. (If that were the case I failed this test a long time ago!) I'm talking about being the keeper of your home. Dads are awesome, husbands are amazing, and none of us want to do life without them, but when it comes down to it, wives and moms generally make the house run. We're the grease that keeps the wheels of our families running smoothly. I feel confident most men would agree. We ARE important, Moma. And we have a job to do bigger than cooking meatloaf and breaking out the Swiffer duster.

To keep our homes, we must be ready to defend it and protect it from the attacks of the enemy. Don't you sit there for one second and think that your home won't or hasn't been attacked. Maybe you didn't realize it at the time, but it has been. Do you think it's a coincidence that you have a terrible Monday on the job after a breakthrough service on Sunday? Is it just a bad streak of luck when you get home from prayer meeting and your washing machine has flooded your house? Is it just 'life' that you can't seem to find 10 spare minutes to sit down and meditate on God's word? I think not. Our homes are targets. Our marriages are targets. Our husbands, our children are targets. What are we doing about it? For too long I've sat back and chocked it all up to life and just tried to keep pressing on. Too long I've prayed patty cake prayers with my babies, and half-heartedly given my time to the Lord. I'm the keeper of this home and I'm at best giving a mediocre fight for what's inside these four walls. I've not given the enemy much to fight against for a while, and now that ends. I'm ready to take up the armor of God, arm myself with the weapons I've been given, and stand at the door post of my home daring the devil to try and sneak inside.

Your work is important, Moma. Your place is vital, Wife. It's time to open our eyes and hearts to the will of God in our lives. As my friend said this morning, Mama Bear ain't playin! Too long I've tiptoed around in my home, timidly praying that things would turn around and that God would plant a love for Him in my children's hearts and protect them. Let me ask you, if you and I were to slip into the woods and try to attack a bear cub, what would happen to us? Do you think Mama Bear would just sit quietly by and watch us sneak up on her baby? Um, I think not. To say she would roar in defense of her own would be an understatement. She would fiercely protect her babies from whatever we brought against them. Against you and I, she would win. There's no contest that in 'hand to hand' combat that Mama Bear would rip us to shreds. She has the upper hand. But what if you and I became the Mama Bear? We know that we are victorious. The Bible tells us that we are MORE than conquerors. He who is in us is greater than the one in the world. Against the enemy that tries to slip in and attack our families and our children, WE have the upper hand. WE have the power of prayer to open up all of Heaven in our defenses. When the devil attacks your family, Mama Bear. When he tries to come against your children, Mama Bear. When he tries to sneak in and steal the joy and peace from your home, Mama Bear. When he tries to convince you that you won't ever see you husband, father, or child living for Jesus, Mama Bear. Ladies, it's time to rise up and get the Mama Bear mentality. We have to stop backing down. We have to stop using paper plate shields against the enemy when he's coming at us with fiery darts. We have to stop being on the defense and get on the offense. Before he makes a step inside your home or your family, slam the door shut on his foot! Roar up in righteous indignation at the very idea that he could come in and take what God has clearly given. God ordained us to be women, wives, mothers, daughters. We are the keeper of our homes. We are fervent, powerhouses of prayer and glory from Heaven. We are defenders of our blessings.

We are Mama Bear.

"Strength and honour are her clothing; and she shall rejoice in time to come. She openeth her mouth with wisdom; and in her tongue is the law of kindness. She looketh well to the ways of her household, and eateth not the bread of idleness. Her children arise up, and call her blessed; her husband also, and he praiseth her."

Proverbs 31:25-28 KJV

30
NOT TODAY, SATAN!

I was listening to our church's praise team playlist on Spotify this morning and the first song that came on pricked my heart. The lyrics to the chorus talked about becoming what God had called the singer to be, and how this was his passionate desire. At one point the lead singer said he wouldn't run from what God has called him to be. That wrenched my heart. For several weeks I've felt disconnected and flatlined in my prayer life, my Bible reading, my relationship with God. It was there, it wasn't totally dead, but it wasn't thriving and beating the way it should be. Honestly today was the first day I've turned worship music on and just listened. Just let my heart open up to those little places where I've been cutting corners and trying to sweep spiritual dust under the rug. How often have I run from what God called me to be and do? If in no other form than to put off fervent and specific prayer, and to be content with reading a chapter or two in my Bible rather than actually studying His word and applying it to myself.

While it's true we go through seasons in our growth, I can't blame lack of participation by me on a dormant season. I can't blame God for being a thousand miles away if I haven't invited Him in lately. How can I wonder why He isn't here if I haven't been speaking to Him and asking Him to come visit with me? I read something recently that said if the devil can't cause us to sin or turn around, then his next job is to distract us. How good he is at that job! While I loathe to give him any credit, it doesn't do me any good to be unaware of the adversary I'm up against. By distracting me and keeping my mind and heart filled with things of this life, he's managed to get my mind and heart off of God. Really, he provides the distraction and I do the rest. If I'm not daily crucifying my flesh and filling myself with the meat of the word, and spending time with my Father in prayer, then it's no wonder I feel disconnected. If I never spoke to or spent time with my husband, what a huge hole that would put in our relationship. A relationship requires give and take on both ends and the same applies to my relationship with God. I can't expect to take if I'm never giving.

I don't know why all this is pouring out. Maybe someone else needs to read it and know they're not the only one who's ever found themselves in a place of disconnect in their spiritual life. Perhaps I just need to get it out in the open so I can see where I'm lacking and improve. Just as my physical belly gets hungry when I go without food, so does my spiritual hunger grow when I fail to give my spiritual belly the nutrients it requires.

I heard it once that you should never lose your song, and that has always stuck with me. I'm a singer. I always have been. I don't think there was ever a time I didn't love music and singing. Nothing gets my worship going more than when I'm singing praises to God. While I may not have the greatest voice, it's a big one that I've dedicated to the One who gave it to me. Losing my song is the thought that came to me while that worship song on Spotify was playing. When I let my spiritual sacrifices slack, my worship slacked with it, and my song became silent. There's a big ole BUT right here though. BUT the greatest thing in all of this is that God still loves me. His love for me is perfect and never ending. His grace is deeper and wider than the ocean and He never left me even when I was shutting the door on Him and the work He was trying to do in me. So though I've been a slacker, God still loves this slacker and He has grace for me. Grace to forgive my shortcomings and help me to be better today than I was yesterday; to be better tomorrow than I am today.

Today I will pick my song back up and deny the enemy any room to distract me, slow me down, or trip me up. While he may have gotten a very tiny victory, I will win this war. His favorite playground is in the mind of you and me, but today I'll take that back. Spiritually speaking, I'm going to waltz into the enemy's camp and take back what he stole from me: my peace, my song, my worship, my focus. I'll end this very impromptu blog with my favorite saying:

Not today, Satan. Not today.

31
DEAR JOB

Dear Job,

This letter finds itself written so many years after your story was written. I've started it in my head more times than I can count. Today I have finally put my words into writing. I know that day probably started so normal, the day your troubles started. In my mind I think you had no warning of what was to come. Truly, you were on the mountaintop one moment and in the valley the next. Did you know that thousands of years later someone would look to you to make it through their own valley? Probably not. But we do. I do. Sometimes I think your story was written out just to remind me that I can keep going, that I'm blessed regardless of my circumstances, and that all I have was given by God and belongs to Him.

You see, Job, life is tough. Of course your story tells us that you know that. Even this many years and generations later, life is not easy. The devil still roams around looking for people to stumble, and ways to bring down the best of us. I can't compare myself to you in regards to your righteousness, I don't think that highly of myself. Mostly, I'm a weak ole human whose flesh wars with my spirit, and wins all too often. Still, your story inspires me. I've had some struggles that you yourself experienced. Money is low, bills are high. Sickness comes time and again. Stress and anxiety flicker at the edges ready to jump in and take over my mind. Isn't that the devil's favorite play place? Of course, you already know. There was no area of your life, other than life itself, that he didn't wreak havoc in.

It's here that I have to state our differences. I've still got my children. I've got my husband. We're all healthy. My husband has a job. We have a home and a vehicle. So though times have been hard, everything hasn't been stripped from me like it was from you. Yet here I am, wondering how I'm going to go up this mountainside, when you yourself kept going. Did you know that you would be a reminder to me that God is more than enough? Could you possibly have known then that your pain would reflect through the ages and bring hope to those feeling hopeless? Oh to have your grace, your faith! I'm working toward those, Job. It's a daily struggle, but one I'm not willing to give up on.

42 chapters. That's how long your story is. You suffered and hurt and although you stumbled, you never gave up. You never bowed to the pressure. You glorified God in your misery. Talk about inspiration! You said one thing that has become ever popular, and which still resonates with my soul. It's a constant firm reminder that God is in control, and His plans are far better than my best laid ones. You said,

"Though he slay me, yet will I trust in him: but I will maintain mine own ways before him." (Job 13:15)

Your faith has brought me through many a dark day, Job. Those words have been a beautiful testament to God's faithfulness to us when we are faithful to Him. So today is hard. You remind me that life wasn't ever meant to be easy, but that doesn't discount God's goodness. I'm blessed more than I deserve, so how can I possibly be upset when things get tough? Your circumstances didn't lessen the greatness of the Almighty, and mine don't either. Do I know how my story will end? Not anymore than you knew how yours would. What I do know is that God is faithful, and the same power He had in your story is the same might He has today in mine. I may not come through as gracefully, Job, but I'm trying. I'm going to try harder today than I did yesterday.

Thank you for your story. I know you had no idea then how much you would impact us today. That's something else your story does for me. It reminds me that my own life is a testament to God's goodness. Somewhere down the line, maybe even today, someone will be watching me. They're going to watch my life, my actions and reactions. I don't want my story to be one that causes others to turn their backs on God, believing He's only good when life is good. I want my story to inspire others like yours does for me. I want them to see resilience during the storm, God's greatness and might in restoring things that looked broken and hopeless. I want to be a story that lives on far after the storm is over. Thank you for your story, Job. Your suffering was not in vain, and your story was not without cause. You brought hope to people, and gave glory to God. I say your story is one worth reading and telling. ❤

32
WE'RE ALL A HOT MESS

In case you're wondering, I do not have it all together. I am, in simple terms, a hot mess. Constantly I run late, forget things, take my kids to church with dirty faces, have dirty dishes piled in the sink, forget to make time to pray, etc. The list could go on and on. Right now there are cookie crumbs in my truck and candy wrappers on my couch. Yesterday it took 10 minutes of hard thinking to remember what day I had last washed my hair.

However, that's not always what I share on Facebook or Instagram. In the interest of putting my best foot forward, I don't always put my inconsistencies out there for the world to see. But that doesn't mean I don't have them. If all you knew about me was my blog or my profile pictures, you might assume that I am a well to-do, have my life together kind of gal. I'm trying not to laugh out loud at the thought of those words describing me. (I'm sure my friends are shaking their heads in agreement, as they know I'm a crazy lady.)

Maybe you don't know where I'm going with this, so I'll tell you. Don't look at part of my life and think you know the whole story. The same goes for myself. I can't creep someone else's Facebook page and be secretly jealous of their perfect house, gorgeous family photo, new car, and adorable picket fence. Chances are, they're just as crazy as me. Well, maybe close anyway. We don't know everyone's story. We don't know how many times this week they forgot to pack their kids lunch box, or if that amazing living room in their last post was the only clean room in their house. Furthermore, we don't know if they had their house spotless because they're having to sell it due to a job layoff. We don't know the struggles behind every shiny smile and seemingly perfect photo.

We can't look at each other and wish we had more. More often than not, we wouldn't want the struggle that comes with that gain. The bottom line here is this: we're all in this together. We're all a hot mess at one time or another. We need prayer partners and friends to help us through the bad times and rejoice with us in the good times. This isn't a competition of who can do better or have more. At the end of the day, we all just want the same thing, and that's to make it to Heaven. So next time you're feeling down about yourself, call me and I'll tell you about last week when I forgot to wash my husband's socks. Don't keep up with the Jones. Keep up with Jesus and just be friends with the Jones.

33
MARY, DID YOU KNOW?

I know when you read my title it doesn't seem overly original. Most likely it evokes thoughts of what I consider to be one of the most popular and favored Christmas songs played and sung each year. While that's a song I love, my thoughts are a little different than the questions it asks.

I'm curious if Mary really did know. Did she know how hard it would be to be the mother of God? I remember being pregnant with my firstborn, my first son. My nerves were all over the place, my mind filled with a new mother's fears and worries. What if I don't know what to do? What if I can't tell if he's hungry or hurting? Can I be a good mother? Am I ready for this? What if he doesn't like me? A new mother has a million and one questions racing through her mind without the added kink of being pregnant by the Holy Ghost, preparing to birth the Son of God.

Did you know, Mary? Did you know what it would be like? Did you know it was going to be that way, to see your heart outside of your chest, knowing all the while He wasn't yours to keep?

I'm not the most worrisome mother, a helicopter mom I will never be. However, I'm not immune to fears for my children. Truly, having a child is to discover more love and worry than you ever dreamed you were capable of. I think of the future of my children and I wonder if Addison will be a singer like her Moma, if Jase will become a scientist, if Ty will be a teacher. What will they do with their lives? Will they be called into the ministry? Will they go to another country and become missionaries?

Did you know from the beginning, Mary? Did you know that the same Savior you birthed under a cloud of criticism would be yours for such a short time, to be taken from you once again surrounded with mockery? When you first looked at His face, did you already know the end? Did you rock Him to sleep knowing how He would give His life for people who would reject Him?

The Christmas story is so much more than a baby in a manger. The manger was only the beginning. It was the first step toward saving humanity. That baby in your nativity signifies the love of a God for His people, a father for His son, a mother for her son, and the pain and sacrifice that sin demanded.

Did you know, Mary, the extent of what your Son would grow to do, and the perfect Savior He would be? Did you know the pains of motherhood would be so great, and the love so fulfilling? Did you know how demanding the days and how sleepless the nights would be? Could you look at Him and tell that He carried the weight of the world on His shoulders? Did you know then, that He was our hope? Did you know you would one day see Him hanging there on that cross? Did you realize that the pain your Mother's heart would feel would be so great?

I wonder, Mary, did you know?

34
WHAT'S YOUR MINISTRY

This started taking form several days ago. Sunday night my Pastor stepped all over it, and I guess that's what I get for not writing it when it was first laid on my heart. Lesson learned, Lord! It was partially inspired by something I say often, "Mommin' is a ministry". Truly, Mommin' is a ministry. We should never take for granted the powerful position and responsibility the Lord has given us as mothers. That thought took me one step further. What else is a ministry? If I can minister while folding socks, are there any other areas in my little life where I could make a difference? Let me share with you what I came up with as a conclusion.

Mommin' is a ministry.

Going to Wal-Mart is a ministry.

Teaching is a ministry.

Working on an oil rig is a ministry.

Digging ditches is a ministry.

Flipping burgers is a ministry.

Working the bank drive through window is a ministry.

Checking out at the grocery store is a ministry.

Going to the park is a ministry.

Walking through the mall is a ministry.

Being a nurse is a ministry.

Owning your own business is a ministry.

Cleaning houses is a ministry.

Working at the nursing home is a ministry.

Being a friend is a ministry.

Basically, if you have breath in your body, you have a ministry. Matthew 28:19 tells us to 'Go ye therefore, and teach all nations.' Just because we aren't in a foreign country or working in a home missions church doesn't mean we don't have a mission field to work in. Everything we do is a ministry. Every place we go is a mission field. We never ever know who we may come in contact with or what they're going through. That's why 2 Timothy 4:2 advises us to be instant in season AND out of season. None of the things I listed above as ministries actually take place in the church or during a church service. So often we get caught up in our ministries being what we do at church or on the platform. While those things are absolutely ministries and absolutely vital, we cannot let our lights dim when we walk out of the church house. Our entire lives were meant to be a ministry, glorifying God. I want to be a light to someone and point them to the church, and to do that I must first BE the church. That may be in Wal-Mart while I'm wrestling my three kids away from the candy display and I least expect it. I've got to be instant in my ministry. Maybe the next time you go shopping and sit down for lunch the person next to you may start making sideways glances at you, wondering what it is about you that they're drawn to. Maybe the next time you buy groceries and the girl checking you out charges you double by mistake, the person in line behind you will see your Christ-like attitude and wonder why you didn't blow up.

We all have a ministry. We all have a mission field. We all have something to bring to the table. We all have amazing opportunities to point others to Jesus. We just need to remember that it doesn't have to be Sunday night with the praise team jamming. We don't have to be the praise team to have a ministry. We don't have to be a preacher. We're all called to be ministers of this Gospel, to be His hands and feet. We need only to realize the full potential of our own personal mission field.

35
WHO'S PRAYING FOR THEM?

I had another thought coming together and I had planned to write it today. My heart, however, seems to have different plans. Do you ever get down to pray and somewhere in the midst of those prayers, you feel like your heart is breaking? That's where I am today. I don't always make time to pray like I should. That's just me being transparent. I have kids and a husband and laundry and a list of excuses a mile long that I could rattle off. Truth is, I just don't MAKE the time. It isn't going to always happen easily. I've got to make it happen. Today is a perfect example of how prayer, when I make that time for it like I should, can change me, and mold me into more of what God wants.

What started as thanks, blended into prayers for lost loved ones, and I admit, I got hung up after that. I got stopped by tears that hit me out of nowhere over souls. Young souls, to be exact. The souls of some young people that I had the pleasure of coming in contact with. Young people who don't have a choice in a lot of things in life, but who loved Jesus. The thought of them never stepping foot back in a church was more than I could handle. At that point, all I could do was just ask God to keep them, to keep His hand on them, and to trust that He had a plan. What really got me, and gets me now, is thinking of all the souls out there that need that prayer. Who's praying for them? Who's weeping for them? Is anyone? How often do I answer the call to prayer by the lost and dying world I see every day? Who's praying for them?

When I was living in sin, I know I had a Moma praying for me. I had a pastor and his wife who never gave up on me. Not everyone has that. Some people don't have a praying Moma or Mamaw like you and I do. They may have never come in contact with a church family and pastor. They may not have a youth leader, a quiz coach, a Sunday School teacher, or puppet/drama leader they can fall back on, even years down the road, and depend on their prayers. If they don't, who's praying for them? I heard a message once that asked the question, When was the last time you wept over your city? Today I'm asking myself, "Tiffany, when did you last weep over someone else's soul? When did you last pray earnestly for the lost souls in your city and community? If all your prayers from today came true tomorrow, who would be affected? Who's praying for them, Tiffany?"

I'll be honest here and say that my prayers are not always where they should be. If I made a list of prayer warriors, my name wouldn't be anywhere near the top. But I try, and today conviction and sorrow are overtaking me. Who's praying for them? If not me, if not you, then who? Why am I really here? I pray all the time for God to help me be a light and a witness, but when did I last weep over a soul? Isn't that part of being a light? Do I always have to be standing there inviting someone to church to be a minister in this world? How can I substitute anything for sincere, earnest, heart wrenching prayer?

The answer is: I can't. I can't coast through life without ever having my heart broken for someone. I'm not here merely to exist, I'm here to lead people to Jesus, to further His kingdom, to bring glory to HIM. I've heard it said time and again that battles are fought on our knees. The battle against sin, death, Hell, and for young people I may never see again is fought on my knees. Ask yourself, who's praying for that lady you saw in the grocery store? That little boy that rode the church van Sunday morning, who's praying for him? Your co-worker, your banker, the homeless man, your dr, your vet, the people we pass every day on the highways and byways, who's praying for them?

My heart broke for a group of young people this morning. Then it broke again when conviction of prayer fell on me. I can't let myself get so caught up in the things of this life that I forget my purpose. My purpose isn't to have the biggest house, the nicest car, the best job, the prettiest clothes, or to be the most popular. My life is meant to live for Jesus, to point others to Him, and to have my heart broken for the things that break His heart. How His heart must break at the multitudes of people who have no one weeping for their souls! I'm sure I've broken it more than once by my lack of prayer and concern for souls.

My post today may be nothing more than my own rambling words to myself. That's ok. A month or a year from now when I go back and read it again, I pray my heart breaks all over again as I wonder, who's praying for them?

36
JESUS, BRING THE RAIN

I found myself singing a song today as I vacuumed, of all things. It just rose up in my spirit and I felt I should share what I was feeling. This song, Jesus, Bring the Rain, by Mercy Me, is a beautiful one and I've always loved it. I admit, I haven't always taken the words straight to heart. It basically asks God to send the good, but if that's not His will, then send the rain. It's in the rain that we grow. Though I may not be in the eye of a storm right now, I've been there many times and no doubt I'll be there again. How many times have I been standing in the pouring down rain, gazing up at Heaven, wondering why the rain continues to fall and the sun never shines?

Looking back at those days of rainfall, I realize I was asking the wrong questions. I was asking, why the rain? When will it end? Where is the sun, my joy? Why don't you lift these clouds the way I know you're able to? All the while I should have been asking, How can this bring You glory? What are You trying to teach me? Who might I be able to teach when I come through this storm? How can I take this pain and use it to reach someone else also experiencing it?

No rain is without reason. Even now as I look out the window, the rain falls in the physical at my house. I personally don't need this rain. I've got enough mud holes to last until next May. But someone may need it. Perhaps a farmer for his crops or a cattlemen for his livestock. I don't know who may need the rain, all I know is that I don't need it. To be honest, I would go so far as to say I didn't want it either. Why do I need rain when I've had my share? Sound familiar? Even in the spiritual, oftentimes I don't want more rain because Tiffany doesn't need it. I don't feel it's beneficial to me in any way, so I grumble and question and begrudge the very thing that may be vital for me to help someone who does need it. Maybe I need the rain and I just don't realize it.

The point is, we can't see all and we don't know all. When the rain is falling, I don't always know the reasons why. I don't know if it's for me, to strengthen my faith, or if it maybe a storm to teach me to be sensitive to someone else who is hurting. Only God knows the reasons. One thing is for certain, He DOES know the reason. Not one raindrop falls that He didn't know about or tell it to fall. Your rainy season isn't punishment, or without a purpose. Every drop is part of His plan. Maybe it's to bring Him glory, as someone looks at you still standing after enduring the storm of a lifetime. What more could I ask for, than for my life to bring glory to my Father? After all, isn't that what our lives are for, to give glory to Him?

I don't know who might read this. Most likely I won't personally know every person who comes across my words. I don't know what each of you are going through. But someone is going through the rain, and you need to know that it's not without purpose, without rhyme or reason. Don't fight your rain clouds, embrace them and ask how your rain can bring Jesus glory. Maybe it won't end today, or tomorrow, and you may not be able to look back any time soon and see the reasons, but one day you will. Don't be discouraged! Hold on and remember that every season has a purpose, and that rain is required to produce growth

37
CLANGING CYMBAL, ANNOYING DISTRACTION

A wise lady told me recently that if I'm confused about whether I should publish something, the answer is probably yes! God is not the author of confusion, but we know who IS a lover of confusion and distraction. So with all that said, I'm going to share with you something that has been on my heart, and in my notebook, for a while now.

"If I speak with the tongues of men and of angels, but have not love [for others growing out of God's love for me], then I have become only a noisy gong or a clanging cymbal [just an annoying distraction]."
1 CORINTHIANS 13:1 AMP

I don't want to be an annoying distraction to others. I don't want to be that stumbling block because I didn't have love. Not just love for others, but love like Jesus that gives me patience and sincerity. I want love that helps me to see the best in everyone and everything. The kind of love that gives me the blinders to overlook mistakes and failures, that helps me stand when times get hard. 1 Corinthians tells us that love isn't easily provoked, love doesn't get angry easy and isn't 'overly sensitive'. How much easier my life could have been at times if I had simply not been so sensitive! Combine that with seeing the good in every circumstance and I could have avoided much turmoil and discontentment. If I'm not full of love through Christ, then I can't avoid these things and I'm nothing more than a clanging cymbal, an annoying distraction.

That part really puts this in a new perspective for me. I know what annoyances are. I know what distractions are. I never thought to link the two together to compare a heart without love. What kind of light or witness can I be if I'm an annoying distraction because I haven't let the love of Christ infiltrate the darkest corners of my heart and life? Love isn't always easy. You hear that when you're getting married or at a tough time in a marriage. You go into marriage and having children understanding that love isn't easy and it doesn't come free. Sometimes it hurts, and that costs us. It costed our Savior everything on Calvary. The one common factor you're always told is this: love is always worth it. Striving to love others like Jesus loves you may not always be easy, and sometimes it may even hurt, but it will always be worth it. It's never wrong to love someone or to apply love to your life. What situation are you in that could be dramatically changed by adding a little love to the mix? How could our attitudes be improved and more joy felt if we applied a little more love? Perhaps we could slip on those proverbial rose colored glasses- the ones tinted by love. What could we see then? Could we see a hurting heart lashing out? Could we feel peace toward a situation that we've been struggling with? Maybe we could see God's hand moving in ways we couldn't see before because we were so far from love that anger and bitterness consumed us.

Reading 'The Love Chapter' in the amplified translation of the Bible has opened my eyes to what love really is. It doesn't just begin and end with having love and kindness and consideration for each other. It goes so much deeper than that! It extends to actively applying the love of Christ to our lives. When we consciously choose to love the way God loves, it changes our entire outlook. It shifts the way we see circumstances and situations. Even more, it changes the way we respond in those situations. Love applied is the deciding factor between responding with understanding and patience, or simply reacting in anger and hurt. It helps us to look over the little things that before would have caused us anxiety or hurt feelings. We begin to focus more prayer on how we can help the situation, rather than the wrong we feel has been inflicted on us or the unfairness.

Maybe no one else will see the revelation here that I got. It was absolutely life changing for me. I want to strive to cover every thought, word, deed, action, reaction, response, situation, and circumstance with the love that God has so often shown to me. I'm no more worthy of His love than I am the grace and mercy that He consistently shows me. Yet He somehow sees fit to freely give me that love. The least I can do is share the same love that I've been shown, and watch as it changes not only my life, but the lives and hearts of others. I don't want to be without love and become an annoying distraction when I have the power of love in my hands to be so much more. To know the love of Christ, is in turn to be the love of Christ.

38
WAR STANDARD

When the enemy comes in like a flood,

The Spirit of the Lord will lift up a standard!

(Isaiah 59:19)

That verse is part of a song that has been stuck in my head for days. Out of the blue, it popped in there and I haven't been able to get away from it. That word 'standard' kept playing over and over in my head, and I began to wonder about its usage. What standard would the Lord raise up? Surely not the 'standards' of my dress or holiness standards. So, naturally I did what I always do. I turned to Google. Here's what I found: standard also means a military or ceremonial flag carried on a pole or hoisted on a pole.

A standard is what is also called a war flag. These standards were used in battle to represent a unit or regiment. Now let's play back those lyrics again with this new definition of standard. When the enemy comes in like a flood, The spirit of the Lord will lift up a war flag. The spirit of the Lord is instant to let the enemy know what regiment we belong to. During my research on standards, I found that they were large, with bold colors and easily visible. When the Lord lifts up a standard on our behalf against the enemy, He is issuing a very visible warning. We don't have to worry or fear when we feel the enemy closing in and trying to corner us up. The Lord will raise a standard high letting our enemy know that He fights for us!

A battle standard was used to help soldiers keep track of their unit during times of war. If a soldier was for some reason separated from his unit, he could simply look for the standard and know which direction he needed to go. Something I read about this really struck home with me. It said, "To be most effective, a soldier needs to be with his unit." Doesn't that sound just like the importance of our church? We need each other! In reality, we are at war with our enemy, Satan. He wars each of us daily for our souls and the souls of our friends and loved ones. To be the most effective soldiers in this war that we can be, we need to be with our unit. I dare say we must also be unity with them. If our unit is warring within itself, it's distracted from the war outside. Lord, help us not to be distracted by confusion or discord that our enemy loves to use against us to weaken our effectiveness as a unit!

The battle standard was also used to help soldiers see where their group is, and where it's going. When the battle is hard and we feel like we don't know where to turn or the direction to go, we need only look for the standard the Lord has raised for us! The Lord not only raises the standard against the enemy, but He raises it for our benefit. The standard is a reminder that we are not alone, that He is fighting for us. Battle standards were made large and easily visible not only to lead the soldiers, but to inspire them during battle. When the Lord raises up the standard, He's not only showing us the way to go, He's using that standard as encouragement to keep fighting. Isn't that just like God?

I think that my favorite thing I read while studying on battle standards is this: "Or even when encamped, if you wander off for a bit, you know where home is." That touched my heart in so many ways. If you've found that you've wandered farther from the camp than you knew or intended, just look for the standard. The standard is ever flying high to call home those soldiers that have gotten lost or weary during the battle. The standard flies to let you know that home is always there, and your unit is ready to receive you with open arms.

If you're fighting the devil tooth and nail and feel like he's coming in like a flood, look up and see the standard that the Lord is raising. The enemy knows he can't win, and he will only use lies to try and convince you otherwise. If you're feeling overwhelmed or defeated, look to the standard and find encouragement knowing that God is always fighting for us. He fights our battles with us, and He also fights many that we may never know about this side of Heaven. He leads His troops through the battles, but He never leaves them. If you've wandered too far from the camp, the standard is still flying for you. It will ever fly in hopes of bringing home even one soldier that has lost their way. The same standard that flies for those fighting the battle, is the same standard flying for those lost or wandering in the battle. The standard the Lord has raised up is for each of us, wherever we may be. How awesome is our God, that He cares that much about us that He has a purpose and plan for each and every one of us? Wherever we may find ourselves today, there is a standard that has been raised on our behalf, by a God that is fighting for us.

39
STAY OUT OF EGYPT

In the Bible, Egypt always represents the world. If you go back and read in the Old Testament, you'll read a story of a hard fought battle by Moses to free the Israelites from the bondage of Egypt. Pharaoh was determined in his hard heart to keep God's people there. We all know that when one is up against God he won't win, but try he did. See, Pharaoh had held the Israelites captive for so long, he believed they belonged to him. But God's people are God's people no matter how long they've been enslaved, no matter how far they've gone, and no matter how hard the taskmaster fights. Moses fought with the God of Heaven on his side and freed the Israelites from their shackles, yet how far did they get before they were looking back into Egypt wondering if they should have stayed? Their every need was attended to and yet they constantly compared walking in freedom to being chained to Pharaoh in a land they were never intended to be in.

The same is true with the church today. Jesus died freely on that cross, fighting Hell and overcoming the grave that we might be free. Then we turn around and follow the model the Israelites set before us and constantly look back at the world, and the things in it, comparing the freedom of Christ with the bauble encrusted shackles we left behind in Egypt. Why would we want to go back there? Why do we long to go back to what we were called out of? Why do we push the boundaries of freedom, trying to fit in and look and act like Egypt when we were called to be set apart? I Peter 2:9 clearly tells us that we were never meant to fit in:

But ye are a chosen generation, a royal priesthood, an holy nation, a peculiar people; that ye should show forth the praises of him who hath called you out of darkness into his marvelous light.

We are a chosen people. We are meant to be peculiar. Why? Because we are set apart as God's people, to give praise to Him. Our outward appearance should always be a sign of our separation, but our hearts are also called to be separate. Our outward appearance and our hearts should both line up with God's word and shine light in this dark world. We're chosen and we're free, and that should flow out of us and stand out to those who are still enslaved to Egypt and the devil's lies. Why would we want to rub shoulders with 'Pharaoh' and his taskmasters, when we're called to point others to the freedom we've gifted with? There are people bound in Egypt with shackles they believe can't ever be broken. If we are blending in with Egypt, we will never be a walking testament to the chain-breaking power of Jesus Christ.

The pull of Egypt starts small. Maybe we don't even realize the hold it already has on us. It's not a big thing, not a Heaven or Hell issue. Rest assured, every longing in your heart that comes from gazing into Egypt has already begun to shackle your heart back to the sins Jesus Christ gave His life to free you from. Why trade a life of joy and peace for one of bondage, fear, and despair? Bondage in sin brings confusion and misery that we were never meant to live in.

How hard it was for the Israelites to escape the clutches of Pharaoh! They had been dependent on him for so many long years that breaking his chains was not an easy process. It's the same when we look back at the world we were delivered from. If we ever take a step back toward Egypt, the steps to Egypt are easier than the steps away. It's easy to walk toward sin, it's harder to walk out. If the Israelites had decided to trade their freedom and go back to the toils of Pharaoh, God would have let them. God gives us freedom of choice. He gives us all we need in Him, including His grace and love, but He won't force us to stay. Freedom isn't freedom if it's forced. Think about that. If you find it hard to walk away from the world, are you really free? Can one be free when their 'freedom' has them bound with chains so tight they can't take one step without a fight?

Your enemy doesn't want you to be free. He wants to keep you so bound that all you see is despair, just as Pharaoh did the Israelites. They couldn't see a way out, and your enemy wants to keep you the same way. He doesn't want you to find freedom in the God that defeated him! He wants you completely enslaved to him. His so-called freedom is a smoke screen covering his lies and deception. The beauties of Egypt will never be worth the trade of joy in Christ. We have to stop looking at Egypt, wishing. We need to keep our eyes on Christ and our freedom in Him for this reason: the shiny things that we long for in Egypt today, will have us chained to walls of hopelessness tomorrow.

....

40
I MISS MY TIME WITH YOU

I was watching a YouTube video of Because of the Times some months back and heard Sis. Mickey Mangun singing a song titled, 'I Miss My Time With You'. Since then, that phrase routinely finds its way to my head and heart. When I miss my time of prayer, does God miss His time with me? Do I have a special time set aside each day for Him? This man that gave His life, this God that gave His son so that I could go free, do I make room for Him in my daily life?

So often I think of Adam, after he and Eve had eaten of the forbidden fruit. Genesis tells us that during the cool part of the day, God came to the garden looking for Adam. Perhaps that was their time. Maybe that was the time of the day they had set aside to commune with one another, the Creator and His creation. A time set apart of the other duties and doings of the day, meant to further the relationship between the two. God expected to find Adam there, and called out to him when he wasn't at the expected place at the expected time. I wonder, does He call me when I skip our time? Or does He call and I've gotten so distracted by the events of the day, or by the notifications on my phone, that I don't hear Him calling out?

As a mom of three, alone time isn't something I get a lot of. If I do, it's early in the morning or late at night. For me, I feel like there's always something that needs to be done that is pulling at me and demanding my attention. (Usually an irate child pulling my skirt tail!) Life is so busy in the world we live in, even for a stay at home mom like myself. But I can't forget to prioritize and set aside a time for my Heavenly Father. A time of prayer and communion with Him is vital to keeping my relationship with Him alive and thriving. How can I expect to waltz into the prayer room on Sunday and have an instant connection if He hasn't heard my voice since the Wednesday before? I've used the analogy before that if I didn't make time for my husband, or vice verse, our marriage would end up in the ditch pretty quickly. We can't just assume we know what each other is thinking and feeling. We can't walk around each other, never spending time together, and expect our relationship not to suffer.

The same goes for our relationship with God. We need time with Him. We need prayer, time in the word, and sometimes just quiet to hear Him speak. It's awfully hard to hear Him speak over the roar of Tom and Jerry. It's imperative that I not try to squeeze Him into my agenda, but rather I carve out a place especially for Him. I try to pray in the mornings when I first get up, before any of my children are awake. I brush my teeth, and I pray, even before my coffee. Sometimes while I'm brushing my teeth, it's like I can feel Him there, settling in, waiting on our time together. He meets me there. He's set aside that time to be with me. How could I ever have anything more important to do than sit down with the King of Kings? When I miss my time with Him, my whole day goes awry. I get annoyed easily at small things, I get frustrated and angered when I should have grace. Oh, but when I start my day speaking to, and listening to, Jehovah, it's better than starting with the best cup of coffee your lips have ever tasted. Life is busy. Our worlds get crazy and turned upside down sometimes, believe me, I know! But we must always remember to make time for the only One who can bring us peace, give us clarity, and help us be seasoned with salt and grace, and ready to face the day head on.

41
A 'FORM' OF GODLINESS

"Having a form of godliness, but denying the power thereof: from such turn away."

2 Timothy 3:5 KJV

"Holding to a form of [outward] godliness (religion), although they have denied its power [for their conduct nullifies their claim of faith]. Avoid such people and keep far away from them."

2 Timothy 3:5 AMP

Form- the visible shape or configuration of something; shape, configuration, formation, structure, construction, arrangement, **appearance, exterior,** outline, format, layout, design

After reading and studying up on this verse, over and over I kept seeing the image of a dress form in my mind. A dress form is a dead, hollow, empty thing. It has no breath in it, no life. Clothes are conformed and altered, clipped and twisted, to fit a dress form. Sometimes in the back, they're 'adjusted' until they fit the form they're put on. The form, however, never changes.

The happens when we put on the 'garments', or outer layer, of godliness, but we're dead inside to its power. If we aren't living godliness, talking and walking in holiness, then we don't fit godliness any more than ill-fitting garments fit a dress form, or mannequin. From many angles it may seem to fit just right, hanging naturally, but upon closer inspection we find the nips and tucks where the garments have been altered. We cannot be a hard, unchanging form, making godliness fit is as we are. Rather, we should always be changing and growing in the garments of godliness. Only then can we achieve true godliness.

God's plan for how we should live will never change. His word will never change. We cannot alter it, tucking in some parts and pinning back others so that it fits **us.** We need all of God's words and commandments to live a full, successful life in Him. Victory and freedom are found in submission. When we submit to God's garments, we are changed from the inside out. No longer will we be a dead, hollow form, but we become a living testament and witness of God and His mercy. His glory will shine through us, and then we can truly tap into the power His godliness brings through our submission to His will and way.

ABOUT THE AUTHOR

Tiffany Strebeck is a mother of three from Nebo, Louisiana. She is an avid reader and coffee drinker. She is a member of the praise team at Sandy Lake United Pentecostal Church. She also runs a blog called A Day in the Life of Five.

Made in the USA
Monee, IL
04 August 2021